COLLINS
COBUILD

ENGLISH GRAMMAR EXERCISES

Katy Shaw

THE UNIVERSITY OF BIRMINGHAM

COLLINS
COBUILD

HarperCollinsPublishers

HarperCollins Publishers
77-85 Fulham Palace Road
London W6 8JB

COBUILD is a trademark of William Collins Sons & Co Ltd

© HarperCollins Publishers Ltd 1991
First published 1991
Reprinted 1991, 1992, 1993, 1995, 1996

10 9 8 7 6

ISBN 0 00 370428 9

Page layout and typesetting by eMC DESIGN, Bromham, Bedfordshire
Printed and bound in Great Britain by Caledonian International
Book Manufacturing Ltd, Glasgow, G64

Acknowledgements

The author and publisher would like to express their gratitude to Joy Charnley for
keyboarding the manuscript.

The author and publishers are grateful to the following for permission to reproduce
the extracts on the pages indicated:

P.D. James and Faber and Faber Ltd from Innocent Blood 5-6, 23, 71;
The Estate of the late Sonia Brownell Orwell and Martin Secker and Warburg Ltd
from Animal Farm 8, 76; Edward Arnold Ltd from Where Angels Fear to Tread
by E.M. Forster 8; The Guardian 9-10, 47, 82; Tate Gallery Publications from
The Turner Collection in the Clore Gallery 10; The late Roald Dahl and Michael
Joseph an Penguin Books Ltd from The Soldier from Someone Lie You 11;
The Observer 17, 66; Edward Arnold Ltd from A Passage to India by
E.M. Forster 21, 71; The Estate of the late Sonia Brownell Orwell and Martin Secker
and Warburg Ltd from 1984 34-45; Victor B. Scheffer and Souvenir Press Ltd from
The Year of the Whale 45-46; The Independent 46-47; Richard Allen and The South
London Press 48 (9b); Edwards and Hargreaves Ltd 60; The Estate of C.P. Snow,
reproduced by permission of Curtis Brown Ltd, London from The Masters 65;
Anita Brookner and Jonathan Cape Ltd from Hotel du Lac 71.

Every effort has been made to contact the owners of copyright material. The
publishers apologize for any omissions, and will be glad to rectify these when the
title is reprinted if details are sent.

The Cobuild Series

Founding Editor in Chief   John Sinclair
Editorial Director   Gwyneth Fox

Contents

Introduction

The Collins COBUILD English Grammar has been specially developed for advanced students and teachers of English. This book of accompanying exercises can be used by students working alone or in class, and will provide teachers with lesson material that supports the Grammar closely.

There are exercises for all ten Chapters of the Grammar and for the Reference Section. It is not necessary for students to work through the material sequentially. They can instead select an exercise that deals with a particular problem. Exercises are cross-referenced to the relevant paragraphs in the Grammar, so that students can check the grammar point that is being practised and refer to the lists of common words, where appropriate.

The exercises are varied in format. Most of them have a closed set of answers, which are given in the answer key at the back of the book. However, there are also some 'open-ended' activities, where students can write answers that are true for themselves. These exercises have a star (*) immediately following the cross-reference, to highlight that they are not keyed. Students should ask their teacher or another English speaker to check their answers to these exercises, if necessary.

It is very important to read the instructions to an exercise carefully. In most exercises, the first question includes a model answer, to reinforce the instructions. Space is provided in the remaining questions for students to write their own answers.

I hope the exercises are both useful and enjoyable. I would be pleased to receive comments and feedback from users.

Katy Shaw

1 Referring to people and things

Introduction to the noun group

1 (Paras. 1.1 to 1.13) Describe the words in bold below in grammatical terms.

    a ... the grounds of a sixteenth century **half-timbered** house.   *modifier*

    b ... much of the **work** is taken on part-time or freelance.   ....

    c Give them all the details **and** specifications.   ....

    d He declined to comment on **the** news.   ....

    e **Charing Cross** is used in calculations of distance to and from London.   ....

    f **We** all enjoy good weather, don't **we**?   ....

    g He gave it to **someone** else.   ....

    h It was a big house with **lots of** windows.   ....

    i **These** are the books you asked for.   ....

    j Cars can be rented at almost **any** airport.   ....

Things which can be counted: count nouns

2 (Paras. 1.16 to 1.23) Write the plural of the following singular count nouns.

a	journey	*journeys*	**f**	mouse	....
b	calf	....	**g**	baby	....
c	man	....	**h**	zebra	....
d	mouth	....	**i**	thought	....
e	shellfish	....	**j**	gallows	....

3 (Paras. 1.16 to 1.23) Write the singular of these plural count nouns.

a	watches	*watch*	**f**	rafts	....
b	toads	....	**g**	hovercraft	....
c	women	....	**h**	buses	....
d	countries	....	**i**	grapefruit	....
e	dice	....	**j**	species	....

For more exercises on the plural form of count nouns, see page 89.

Things not usually counted : uncount nouns

4 (Paras. 1.24 to 1.34) Link the sentence openings on the left with appropriate endings on the right, using the verbs below to fill in the gaps. You can use a verb more than once.

be   cause   cook   grow   have   involve   travel

i	Draughts	a	.... not yet come up with a cure.
ii	Mumps	b	.... *is* played on a board with black and white squares.
iii	News	c	.... an illness which is very dangerous to pregnant women.
iv	Genetics	d	.... about 1cm a month.
v	Spaghetti	e	.... vigorous exercise.
vi	Research into cancer	f	.... in about 8 minutes.
vii	German measles	g	.... a swollen neck.
viii	Hair	h	.... fast.
ix	Aerobics	i	.... the study of genes.

i	ii	iii	iv	v	vi	vii	viii	ix
b								

5 (Para. 1.26) Decide which of the sentences on the right are possible. There is more than one correct sentence in each group.

i   What did your teacher do?
    a   He gave me some good advices.
    b   He gave me a good advice.
    c   He gave me some good advice.
    d   He gave me good advice.

ii   How is my English coming on?
    a   You're making a lot of progresses.
    b   You're making a lot of progress.
    c   You're making progress.
    d   You're making a progress.

iii   What do you dislike about living in a big city?
    a   My hairs are always getting dirty.
    b   My hair is always getting dirty.
    c   My hair feel dirty.
    d   My hair feels dirty.

iv   What was her holiday like?
    a   She had an appalling weather.
    b   She had appalling weather.
    c   The weather was fantastic.
    d   The weather were fantastic.

v   Do you like the place where you're staying at the moment?
    a   I haven't got many respects for my landlady.
    b   I haven't got much respect for my landlady.
    c   I have a great respect for my landlady.
    d   I have great respect for my landlady.

vi Why did she get upset?

   a The news were bad.
   b The news was bad.
   c There was some bad news waiting for her.
   d There was a bad news waiting for her.

vii Do you like the room?

   a The furnitures are shabby.
   b The furniture is shabby.
   c There isn't enough furniture.
   d There aren't enough furnitures.

viii What happened when you got to the check-in?

   a Our baggage was overweight.
   b Our baggages were overweight.
   c We had too many baggages.
   d We had too much baggage.

ix Could you lend me £5?

   a Sorry, I haven't got many money.
   b Sorry, I haven't got much money.
   c Sorry, my money's in my room.
   d Sorry, my moneys are in my room.

x Why did you come home so late?

   a The traffic were heavy.
   b The traffic was heavy.
   c There were a lot of traffic.
   d There was a lot of traffic.

Referring to groups : collective nouns

6 (Paras. 1.48 to 1.52) Expand the following newspaper headlines to make a paragraph. The first sentence has been written for you.

LOCAL PRESS CONCERNED ABOUT PRESENT SITUATION

OPPOSITION STRONGLY OPPOSED TO CUTS

STAFF DROP IN MORALE

PUBLIC VERY DISSATISFIED

GOVERNMENT CUTTING BACK ON EDUCATION

LOCAL COUNCIL CLAIM SCHOOLS NOT AFFECTED

LOCAL SCHOOLS DETERIORATING

COMMUNITY UP IN ARMS

FAMILY AFFECTED

The local press is very concerned about
....
the present situation in schools.
....

7 (Paras. 1.49 to 1.52) Choose the most likely alternatives to complete the following sentences.

   a The staff **is/are** united on this issue.

   b The staff **is/are** all here and **is/are** waiting in the staffroom.

   c The council **has/have** agreed to a re-vote.

   d The council **has/have** made numerous improvements in the area.

   e The press **is/are** unreliable as **its/their** source remains uncertain.

   f The press **is/are** outside - you'd better go out the back way!

   g The government **consists/consist** of a number of MPs.

   h The government **is/are** arguing fiercely with **its/their** opponents.

Referring to people and things by name : proper nouns

8 (Para. 1.56) Look at the list of titles in paragraph 1.56 and write four examples from the list in each of the following columns. Two have been filled in for you. You can use the same title in more than one column if you need to.

Family	Honorary titles	Royalty	Church	Hospital	Police	Military
Miss	*Baron*	....	....	....	....	....
....	....	....	....	....	....	....
....	....	....	....	....	....	....
....	....	....	....	....	....	....

Nouns which are rarely used alone

9 (Para. 1.66) Use your Cobuild dictionary if necessary to suggest what extra information you could add to the following nouns. An example has been given.

a   a   ......*vivid*...... impression   e   an   .... rate

b   the   .... world   f   the   .... regime

c   a   .... discovery   g   a   .... version

d   the   .... edition   h   a   .... extent

Referring to activities and processes : '-ing' nouns

10 (Paras. 1.78 to 1.83) Fill in the gaps in the following dialogue between two foreign students in England. The first gap has been completed for you.

Tina :   Are you enjoying life in England?

Paula :   Very much. At the ......*beginning*...... it was strange, but I had the

.... I'd soon settle in, and I was right.

Tina :   I felt the same. At the first .... with the Principal of the school, he gave us

a .... and told us not to spend too much time .... if

we wanted to learn English, so I've tried to study as much as possible.

But .... in my room is difficult when really I'd like to be out

.... – I just love shops!

Specifying more exactly : compound nouns

11 (Paras. 1.84 to 1.93) Complete the following sentences, using the compound nouns in the box below.

air conditioning	compact disc	package holiday
bank account	greenhouse effect	police station
blood pressure	high school	post office
book token	hire purchase	telephone number
brain drain	inverted commas	traveller's cheques
burglar alarm	letter-box	value added tax
car park	modern languages	X-ray

a When you write, you use . . . . *inverted commas* . . . . for direct speech.

b To open a . . . ., please write your name, address and . . . .

and answer all the questions below. We will then send you a cheque book.

c If someone breaks into the house, the . . . . will go off – you'd better call the

. . . .

d If you're feeling run down, ask the doctor to give you a check up - he'll check your . . . .

and he may even ask the hospital to give you a chest . . . .

e We're going to Spain – the travel agent's booked a . . . . for us and we've

already got our tickets and . . . . We'll leave our car in the long stay

. . . . at the airport and the hotel sounds good - it's got

. . . . , so the rooms should be cool.

f He's still at. . . . . , studying. . . . . He has to

read a lot, so he'd probably appreciate a . . . . for his birthday.

g Buy the stamps at the . . . . and pop the letters in the . . . . outside.

h Scientists are very concerned about the results of deforestation, which has contributed to the

. . . .

i The emigration of professionals to better paid jobs abroad is known as the . . . .

j We haven't paid for the . . . . player yet – we've got it on

. . . . – it was £650 plus . . . . , but we're paying

over two years.

Review : The noun group

12 Underline the nouns in the extract below.

Afterwards she had sat on the bed and watched while her mother packed her case. Everything that she had brought with her from prison went in; the suit in which she had travelled to London, her gloves, her underclothes, her shoulder bag, even her toilet articles and pyjamas. It was an extravagance thus to relinquish even the small necessities of living, all of which would have to be replaced; but Philippa didn't check her . . .

Still without speaking Philippa took the case from her mother and hurled it into the middle of the stream. She had first glanced each way to make sure that the tow–path was empty, but even so the splash as the case hit the water sounded so like a falling body that they simultaneously glanced at each other, frightened that someone from the road must have heard.

from Innocent Blood by P.D.James

13 Insert each of the following nouns into the sentences below, and add the appropriate form of the verb in brackets.

advice flock hair knowledge music news progress suburbs trousers

a My parents are both dark, but my . . . . *hair* . . . . *is* . . . . naturally blonde. (**be**)

b The . . . . you gave me . . . . really useful – thank you! (**be**)

c On no! My . . . . ! What can I do? (**split**)

d I'm afraid that the . . . . worse than we'd feared. (**be**)

e The . . . . of most large cities . . . . heavily populated. (**be**)

f The . . . . of sheep in the pen . . . . about 100. (**number**)

g My . . . . of English . . . . gradually – the teacher has told me my

. . . . good. (**increase, be**)

h . . . . really . . . . me relax. (**help**)

Referring to people and things without naming them : pronouns

14 (Paras. 1.94 to 1.114) Explain what each pronoun refers to.

a Have you seen the plane? **It**'s really big. it = *the plane* . . . .

b Husband : The children love **their** presents. their = ...

Wife : Have **you** given **them** to **them** already? you = ...

them = ...

them = ...

c Sue : I'm bringing one of **my** friends tonight. I = ...

my = ...

Helen : Oh? What's **their** name – have **I** ever met **them**? their = ...

I = ...

them = ...

d Steve : No-one's received **their** postcards from our holiday yet. their = ...

Mary : Oh – when did **you** send **them**? Everyone's had **theirs** you = ...

from our holiday – John and I sent **ours** on the first day, them = ...

so **they** got **our** news on the day before **we** got back. theirs = ...

ours = ...

they = ...

our = ...

we = ...

Referring to the subject : reflexive pronouns

15 (Paras. 1.115 to 1.122) Insert a reflexive pronoun, a personal pronoun, or a possessive pronoun into each gap.

a Look at Chris – He cut *himself* while ...*he*.... was shaving.

b The Third World has established .... as a low cost manufacturer.

c The child stared at .... intently in the mirror, realising for the first time that the face was .... own.

d The first time I managed to do it, ... was really proud of .... and .... parents were proud of .... too.

e We couldn't resolve the problem – we asked .... if it was .... own fault.

Referring to people and things in a general way : indefinite pronouns

16 (Paras. 1.127 to 1.140) Fill in the gaps with indefinite pronouns.

We were all sitting watching television the other night. There was ...*nothing*..... interesting on – but we were all tired, so we were willing to watch .... at all, as long as it was .... which would help us relax after a hard day's work. Anyway, after half an hour, a ghost story came on, and we all started watching it. Then .... really started enjoying themselves. It was a gripping story, and .... was really involved in it. When it finished, ... spoke – .... in the room was dead quiet. Then there was a loud thud outside.

Although we were sure .... could be outside the house, ... dared move. Eventually .... went to the window and peered outside. There wasn't .... there. Suddenly there was another noise – this time a crack of twigs. .... wanted to admit how nervous they felt. .... crept towards the back door. Just as we reached it, there was a loud metallic sound, and the cat flap shot open. There had been .... outside, after all – but to .... relief, it was only the cat.

Other pronouns

17 (Paras. 1.109; 1.157 to 1.160) Explain what the pronouns in bold refer to in the following sentences.

a There are two cups – **one** with sugar and **one** without.   one = ...*a cup*.....

                                                                    one = ...

b They made three cakes – **one** was eaten and   one = ...

   the others were left.   the others = ...

c **One** hopes that this situation will improve.   one = ...

7

d I've poured out the coffee – this **one's** for you.   one's = ...

e I saw **one** man pass it to **another**.   one = ...

another = ...

f They both cooked – **one** made an omelette and   one = ...

one a souffle.   one = ...

g They ate, **each** savouring every mouthful.   each = ...

h They used the same recipe book – I don't know which recipe,   one = ...

but it was **one** or **the other** of them.   the other = ...

i They were given a plate **each**.   each = ...

Review : Pronouns

18 (Paras. 1.94 to 1.160) Underline the pronouns in the passages below.

> They had won, but they were weary and bleeding. Slowly they began to limp back towards the farm. The sight of their dead comrades stretched upon the grass moved some of them to tears. And for a little while they halted in sorrowful silence at the place where the windmill had once stood. Yes, it was gone; almost the last trace of their labour was gone!
>
> *from Animal Farm by George Orwell*

> Meanwhile Lilia prided herself on her high personal standard, and Gino simply wondered why she did not come round. He hated discomfort, and yearned for sympathy, but shrank from mentioning his difficulties in the town in case they were put down to his own incompetence.
>
> *from Where Angels Fear to Tread by E.M. Forster*

Identifying what you are talking about : determiners

19 (Para. 1.208) Use determiners from the list in paragraph 1.208 to complete the gaps in the following passage.

A number of people come to Britain every year – ...*many*... visitors come as tourists and .... people come to work here. But whatever .... reason they have, almost .... visitor goes to see .... Changing of .... Guard. This is one of .... greatest attractions in .... capital. Another's .... Tower of London – .... tourist I have ever met has seen it. .... real sightseer would go home without walking around it. .... people walk around it every day and .... of them are dissatisfied with what they see – .... of them return to see it again.

20 (Paras. 1.162 to 1.181; 1.212) Choose the correct alternative in each of the following.

a We're planning to go to **Far East/the Far East** on holiday.

b Dialysis is used for purifying **blood/the blood** if your kidneys don't work properly.

   c I started learning to play **violin/the violin** when I was five.

   d She'd always dreamed of going on **stage/the stage**, or at least working in **theatre/the theatre**.

   e The roof of **church/the church** was blown off in the hurricane.

   f We went to **church/the church** last Sunday, as usual.

   g Members of **government/the government** are most concerned about **economy/the economy** at the present.

21 (Paras. 1.162 to 1.181; 1.212; 1.213 to 1.220) Use 'a', 'an', 'the' or nothing at all to fill the gaps.

   a I got ...*a*.... postcard from Anne yesterday. Sometimes, ... postcards can be boring but .... one she picked out is lovely.

   b She went to .... doctor because she had .... terrible cold, but he said she had .... flu and told her to stay in .... bed.

   c I'd always wanted to play .... piano, so we went out and bought .... old one for .... children and luckily we've managed to get hold of .... fantastic teacher.

   d In .... past, ... lot of time was spent making .... fire to warm .... rooms, but now with .... central heating .... fires are becoming a thing of .... past.

Other determiners

22 (Para. 1.236) Rewrite the following sentences.

   a They asked for £100. She paid £200.

      She .... *paid them twice the sum they asked for.* ....

   b They gave me £50, I'd asked for £100.

      They..

   c Sebastian was enjoying himself. William was enjoying himself.

      Both..

   d His salary was £25,000 a year. Now he's earning £50,000.

      He's..

   e I opened my Christmas presents, so did the children, and so did the rest of the family.

      All..

Review : Determiners

23 (Paras. 1.161 to 1.236) Use determiners to complete these texts. Not every gap will need a determiner.

   a   .*The*. cause of ...... outrage is Mr Feldt's plan to ban ...... strikes and prohibit ...... increases in

...... pay, ... prices, ... dividends and ......
rents for two years. ...... cause of his plan is a wave
of ...... strikes which has pushed ...... inflation
rate up to 6.7%, as ...... consensus system of ......
employers and ...... unions agreeing ...... "going–
rate" has failed to keep ...... rises in ...... line with
...... international levels.

from The Guardian

b .*One*. hundred and thirty–six years after his death Turner's
great gift of ...... paintings has found ...... permanent home in
...... Clore Gallery, ... newly built extension to ...... Tate
Gallery on Millbank. There in ...... splendid suite of ......
rooms ...... entire contents of his studio can be seen arranged
in ...... beautiful and instructive sequence following ......
central themes of Turner's art. ...... book provides ......
readable and accessible introduction to ...... display, and
includes ...... account of ...... collection of ...... works on
...... paper, together with ...... guide to ...... use of ......
Study Room in which they can be examined by ...... public.

from The Turner Collection in the Clore Gallery

24 Insert a pronoun or determiner in each gap.

The large room was full of people. .*One*. of the girls in yellow
was playing the piano, and beside ...... stood a tall, red–haired
young lady from a famous chorus, engaged in song. ...... had
drunk a quantity of champagne, and during the course of ......
song she had decided, ineptly, that everything was very, very sad
– ...... was not only singing, ... was weeping too.
Whenever there was a pause in the song ...... filled ...... with
gasping, broken sobs, and then took up the lyric again in a
quavering soprano. The tears coursed down ...... cheeks – not
freely, however, for when ...... came into contact with ......
heavily beaded eyelashes ...... assumed an inky colour, and
pursued the rest of ...... way in slow black rivulets.

from The Great Gatsby by F.Scott Fitzgerald

2 Giving more information about things

Introduction

1 (Paras. 2.1 to 2.18) Underline all the adjectives in the following excerpt.

Let's have some memories of sweet days. The seaside holidays in the summer, wet sand and red buckets and shrimping nets and the slippery seaweedy rocks and the small clear pools and sea anemones and snails and mussels and sometimes the grey translucent shrimp hovering deep down in the beautiful green water.

from The Soldier from Someone Like You by Roald Dahl

Information focusing : adjective structures

2 (Paras. 2.19 to 2.23) Underline the adjectives, and say whether they are used attributively or predicatively.

a We drew the <u>velvet</u> curtains and put on the light. ....*attributive*..........

b I felt shattered. ....

c He drove the old jeep far too fast. ....

d It was a terribly hard decision to make. ....

e We drank sparkling white wine. ....

Identifying qualities : qualitative adjectives

3 (Para. 2.28) Choose suitable adjectives from this list to complete the sentences below. In some cases there may be more than one alternative.

anxious appropriate attractive busy different difficult easy fine hard patient pleasant

silly simple understanding warm worried

a The road you live in is really ....*busy*......... - I've never seen so many cars.

b He's a really .... and .... man, very .... from anyone else I've met; I find him really ....

c The weather on our holiday was .... and .... - much more .... than I'd expected.

d This exercise is not ...., but it's quite .... to do even .... exercises sometimes - and it's .... to make .... mistakes.

e I'm really .... to get through the exam - although I'm not .... about it - if I give .... answers I should do all right!

Identifying the class that something belongs to : classifying adjectives

4 (Paras. 2.29 to 2.33) Cross out the adjectives which are not possible in this passage.

He lives in an **urban/official** area in **north/northern** England, but originally comes from a **military/rural** part of **south/southern** Scotland. He was brought up in a **traditional/commercial** way, and would like to see more **theoretical/educational** reforms to improve the teaching in our schools. His **active/domestic** involvement in the community is impressive, particularly given his **natural/physical** health. He has unfortunately had to undergo **personal/medical** treatment recently, but is apparently making a **full/regular** recovery.

5 (Paras. 2.29 to 2.33) Decide which of the classifying adjectives in the left hand column go best with the nouns in the right hand column.

i	I collect foreign	**a**	amenities
ii	There are a number of public	**b**	toys
iii	Most of them live in urban	**c**	guitar
iv	He plays the electric	**d**	emancipation
v	She's a single	**e**	areas
vi	He went to medical	**f**	stamps
vii	They fought for female	**g**	school
viii	They were playing with wooden	**h**	parent

i	ii	iii	iv	v	vi	vii	viii
f							

Identifying colours : colour adjectives

6 (Paras. 2.34 to 2.39) Decide which of the following colour adjectives are appropriate. There is more than one possible answer in each case.

i His hair was
- **a** greyish
- **b** whitish
- **c** reddish-brown
- **d** the blackest I've ever seen
- **e** yellowish-black
- **f** bright brown

ii She was wearing
- **a** a scarlet-red coat
- **b** an orangy-red coat
- **c** a deep red coat
- **d** a creamish coat
- **e** a bright black coat
- **f** a pale white coat

iii They had the house painted
- **a** dark white
- **b** pinkish red
- **c** light black
- **d** bright yellow
- **e** yellowy white
- **f** deep purple

Showing strong feelings : emphasizing adjectives

7 (Para. 2.40) Choose an emphasizing adjective from the list in paragraph 2.40 to
fill each of the gaps in the postcards below.

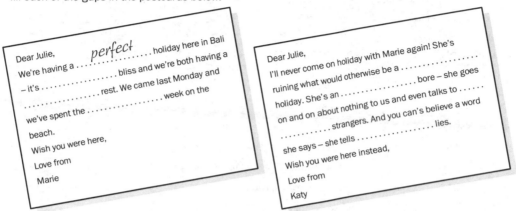

Dear Julie,
We're having a . . . . *perfect* . . . . holiday here in Bali
– it's . . . . bliss and we're both having a
. . . . rest. We came last Monday and
we've spent the . . . . week on the
beach.
Wish you were here,
Love from
Marie

Dear Julie,
I'll never come on holiday with Marie again! She's . . . .
ruining what would otherwise be a . . . .
holiday. She's an . . . . bore – she goes
on and on about nothing to us and even talks to . . . . . .
. . . . strangers. And you can's believe a word
she says – she tells . . . . lies.
Wish you were here instead,
Love from
Katy

Making the reference more precise : post determiners

8 (Para. 2.44) Use the word given in brackets and choose one of the adjectives in
paragraph 2.44 to fill in the gaps below. Use the correct word order.

a He lives on . . . . . *the other* . . . . side of the road. (**the**)

b She has . . . . copies of the manuscript. (**the, two**)

c We outlined . . . . problems. (**our, own**)

d You must try and get . . . . worries off your chest. (**your**)

e The woman had frittered away . . . . fortune. (**her**)

f Freddy was . . . . relative. (**my**)

Special classes of adjectives

9 (Para. 2.46) Complete each of the following sentences by using one of the
adjectives from the lists in paragraph 2.46, together with one of the words below.

congratulations failure glance ideas medicine task teacher village

a His reading was so bad that they asked a . . . . . . *remedial* . . . . *teacher* . . . . . . to help him.

b She trained as a doctor, and then specialised in . . . .

c I see her quite often as she lives in a . . . .

d I stared at it hard but he only gave it a . . . .

e He apologised and wished me . . . .

f His death was caused by . . . .

g I hate cleaning the house - it's a . . . .

h Try not to start the job with . . . .

10 (Para. 2.48) * Complete the sentences below.

 a I am glad . . . .

 b You're welcome . . . .

 c It's unlikely . . . .

 d My best friend was sorry . . . .

11 (Paras. 2.55; 2.57) Use the lists in paragraphs 2.55 and 2.57 to fill in the gaps
in the following sentences, adding 'to' or 'that' as appropriate.

 a He was . . . . *inclined to* . . . . . be moody.

 b She's . . . . work hard.

 c Peter was . . . . they'd pass the exam, but they were . . . .

    they'd fail.

 d It's . . . . rain, just when I wanted to play tennis!

 e If you're . . . . drive, please do.

 f I'm . . . . tell you what I really think, so don't ask me!

Position of adjectives in noun groups

12 (Paras. 2.58 to 2.66) Put the words below in the correct order to complete the
sentences.

   roast/most delicious

 a My mother cooks the . . . . *most delicious roast* . . . . . . beef in the world.

   concrete/grey/modern

 b His father worked in a . . . . building.

   chequered/red and white/pretty

 c On the table was a . . . . tablecloth.

   light brown/straight/ordinary

 d He had . . . . hair.

Special forms - '-ing' adjectives

13 (Para. 2.71) Complete the following extract from a letter using '-ing' adjectives.

I'm absolutely delighted to say that at last I've got a job. I had an interview with a . . . . . *charming* . . . . lady and think the job will be really . . . . - there's a lot to do, so it may be . . . . , but I wouldn't want a job which was . . . . and where there was nothing to do. It's also really . . . . getting something at last - I've had 24 interviews, and a lot of them have been . . . . I was beginning to find being unemployed very . . . . Some of the people I've had interviewing me have been really . . . . - I've felt terrified - and I've found their indifference . . . . It was . . . . to meet someone who was so . . . . - I'm going to feel at home working for her - I'm over the moon!

14 (Paras. 2.74 to 2.79) Choose a suitable noun from the right hand column to follow the sentence openings on the left. Then complete the sentences appropriately. One has been done for you.

i	He made scathing	**a**	work . . . .
ii	He had an overbearing	**b**	remarks . . . . . . *about the size of the room.* . . . .
iii	She was in excruciating	**c**	car. . . . .
iv	She's an enterprising	**d**	house . . . .
v	She hit an oncoming	**e**	experience . . . .
vi	He did outstanding	**f**	victim . . . .
vii	He was the unwitting	**g**	personality . . . .
viii	They've bought an old rambling	**h**	pain. . . . .
ix	It was an uplifting	**i**	snack . . . .
x	It's a really appetizing	**j**	businesswoman. . . . .

i	ii	iii	iv	v	vi	vii	viii	ix	x
b									

15 (Paras. 2.81 to 2.97) Using the word in brackets, rewrite the sentences below keeping the meaning similar.

a She found the situation very interesting. **(intrigued)**

She was intrigued by the situation. . . . .

b The show will almost certainly be a flop. **(destined)**

. . . .

c His only concern is his own problems. **(preoccupied)**

. . . .

d He wasn't in the mood to help us. **(disposed)**

. . . .

e I really owe my parents a lot. **(indebted)**

. . . .

Compound adjectives

16 (Paras. 2.102 to 2.103) Fill in the gaps in the following sentences with compound adjectives from the list in paragraphs 2.102 and 2.103.

a The policeman was wearing a . . *bullet-proof* . . . . . . vest, which probably saved his life.

b Our household has a lot of . . . . devices to make housework easier, and we usually

take advantage of . . . . credit so that we have longer to pay for them.

15

c Their first home was a . . . . flat, and now they're moving to a typical English
. . . . terraced house.

d We try to make good use of . . . . aids in this school.

e I'd rather you didn't make any . . . . phone calls.

f She bought a . . . . car, and it was converted so that it could run on
. . . . petrol.

g The market has been flooded with cheap . . . . toys.

h He could be briefly and accurately described as a . . . . liar.

Comparing things : comparatives and superlatives

17 (Paras. 2.108 to 2.127) Say whether the adjectives in bold are **comparative** or
superlative.

a I'm much **taller** than you.   *comparative*
. . . .

b We moved to a **bigger** house than we had had before.   . . . .

c It was **the cheapest** ring I had ever bought.   . . . .

d She gradually became **calmer**.   . . . .

e The film was **the most exciting** one I had seen for ages.   . . . .

f This cake is **better** than the last one you made.   . . . .

g Food became **more plentiful** each day.   . . . .

h That is **the most important** part of the job.   . . . .

18 (Paras. 2.108 to 2.116) Rewrite the sentences below using the comparative
form of the adjectives in brackets.

a Motorways are wider than country lanes.
Country lanes . . . . *are narrower than motorways.* . . . . (**narrow**)

b I am a lot younger than my brother.
My brother . . . . (**old**)

c Billy is much taller than Sam.
Sam . . . . (**short**)

d The village pond is twice as deep as the swimming pool.
The swimming pool . . . . (**shallow**)

e Joe's suitcase is lighter than Mike's.
Mike's . . . . (**heavy**)

19 (Paras. 2.117 to 2.127) Insert the superlative form of these adjectives into the extracts from an article on Record Breakers. You can use an adjective more than once.

cold dry great heavy high hot long low wet windy

FROM THE HARD RAIN TO THE BIG CHILL

Although the British climate is hitting new extremes, it is not yet in world record class. The giant hailstones of Coffeyville, Kansas still remain unchallenged.

GREATEST . . . . SNOWFALL (over 12 months) :
At Paradise, Mt. Rainier, Washington, USA, 1,224.5in/110.2cm fell between 19 February 1971 and 18 February 1972.

. . . . HAILSTONES :
 Coffeyville, Kansas USA was bombarded with 1.67lb/750g hailstorm on 3 September 1970. They measured 7.5in/19cm in diameter and 17.5/44.45 cm in circumference.

. . . . PLACE (annual mean) :
Turunendo, Colombia receives around 463.4in/1,177 cm of rain each year.

. . . . PLACE (annual mean) :
The Atacamba Desert near Calama, Chile has the grand total of zero rainfall in an average year. The Atacamba area suffered a drought for 400 years - . . . . drought on record - which ended in 1971.

. . . . SHADE TEMPERATURE :
Al'Aziz ayah, Saudi Arabia, recorded 58C/136.4F on 13 September 1922.

. . . . PLACE :
Dallol, Ethiopia had an annual mean temperature of 34.4C/94F between 1960 and 1966.

. . . . PLACE :

. . . . measured mean temperature at Plateau Station, Antartica is -56.6°C/-70°F.

. . . . SURFACE WIND SPEED :
Mt. Washington, Massachusetts, USA was buffeted by winds of 231 mph/371 kph on 12 April 1934.

. . . . PLACE :
Gales regularly reach 200 mph/320 kph in Commonwealth Bay, George V Coast, Antarctica.

Modifying using nouns : noun modifiers

20 (Paras. 2.174 to 2.179) Choose the best alternative in each of the following sentences.

   a I put my keys in my **trouser pocket / trousers pocket**.

   b Many people are arguing against the **arm race / arms race**.

   c I asked her to sharpen the **scissor blades / scissors blades**.

   d Where did you put the **binocular case / binoculars case**?

   e I washed my **jean belt / jeans belt** by mistake.

   f They have reported **troop movement/troops movement** close to the border.

Possessive structures

21 (Paras. 2.180 to 2.192) Insert apostrophes in the appropriate places.

   a Ive got a brother and two sisters. My brothers teacher at St Marys School was Miss Williams, and my sisters was Mrs James.

   b Miss Williams hair was grey, unlike Mrs Jamess, which was red.

   c My brother-in-laws car is not as fast as my friends new car.

   d We saw the sheeps tails disappear behind the barn as the dogs chased them.

   e Small shops prices are usually higher than supermarkets ones.

Talking about quantities and amounts

22 (Paras. 2.195 to 2.210) Complete the gaps below using these quantifiers. You can use each one more than once.

a good deal of a great deal of heaps of lots of the majority of many of
a number of a quantity of some of tons of the whole of

   a There was .... *a great deal of* ... concern about energy shortages.

   b .... people eat .... bread.

   c I couldn't believe it - the children ate absolutely .... food at the party!

   d He's devoted .... work towards producing .... fresh vegetables.

   e .... the refugees have enough to eat, but .... them have very little.

   f There were quite .... delegates at the conference.

   g Don't worry, you've got .... time!

   h We spent .... the summer gardening, and managed to do .... work.

Talking about amounts of things : other partitives

23 (Paras. 2.211 to 2.224) Choose one noun to fit each partitive structure.

beer butter dirt evidence flour glass grass honey lemon rubbish salt whisky

a a grain of ..... *salt* ....   **g** a barrel of ....

b a sheet of ....   **h** a sack of ....

c a knob of ....   **i** a tumbler of ....

d a clump of ....   **j** a speck of ....

e a heap of ....   **k** a shred of ....

f a blob of ....   **l** a dash of ....

24 (Paras. 2.217 and 2.218) Choose a suitable partitive for each of the following nouns.

a a ..... *basket* ......of fruit   **f** a ....of beer

b a ....of petrol   **g** a ....of potatoes

c a ....of milk   **h** a ....of margarine

d a ....of toothpaste   **i** a ....of chocolate

e a ....of medicine   **j** a ....of jam

25 (Para. 2.222) Define the following nouns.

a chair. *A chair is a piece of furniture.* ....

b suitcase...

c dress ....

d news story..

Talking about age

26 (Paras. 2.275 to 2.280) Rewrite the following sentences.

a He's more than 30 years old and less than 40 years old.
He's in . *his thirties.* ....

b Her father is nearly 80.
He's in ....

c She's about 41 or 42.
She's in ....

d His sister's 16 and he's 14.
They're in...

Approximate amounts and measurements

27 (Paras. 2.281 to 2.288) Write the following in full sentences.

 a there / be / roughly 800 / student / my school
 There are roughly 800 students in my school. . . . .

 b approximately / $^1/_2$ them / live / town / $^1/_2$ / country
 . . . .

 c something like / 20% / live / farms / and / nearly all fathers / grow / crops
 . . . .

 d surrounding farms / be / 800 years old / thereabouts
 . . . .

 e there/ be / more than / 200 farms / around / town
 . . . .

 f local population / roughly / 3000
 . . . .

Review of quantities and amounts

28 *Write six sentences, each containing one of the following. Look at the example below.

 a carton of   a couple of   a flock of   most of   much of   a pool of
 . . . *He met her a couple of years ago.* . . . .

Nouns with prepositional phrases

29 (Para. 2.305) Choose an appropriate noun from the lists in paragraph 2.305 and add a suitable preposition to fill in the gaps in the following sentences.

 a His car was involved in a terrible . . . . *collision* . . . . *with* . . . another vehicle.

 b She made a generous . . . . the collection.

 c The child has a great . . . . mathematics.

 d He expressed absolute . . . . the inadequate teaching he had received.

 e The government placed an immediate . . . . all imports from that country.

 f The man had made adequate . . . . his family in his will.

 g He bears a terrible . . . . the people who attacked him.

 h On that point I'm in . . . . Mr McCabe.

 i This requires a . . . . public spending.

 j Will the U.N. . . . . whaling accomplish anything?

Nouns with non-finite clauses

30(Para. 2.316) Fill in the gaps with suitable nouns from the list in paragraph 2.316.

a I'd love the ..... *chance* ..... to go to England this year.

b She showed a great .... to work.

c An .... to type is an advantage.

d I haven't had the .... to tidy my room this week.

e If you can do this, you have no further .... to worry about your English!

Review : Giving information about people and things

31Underline all the adjectives in the excerpt below, and circle all the expressions used to refer to measurements or quantities.

The caves are readily described. A tunnel eight feet long, five feet high, three feet wide, leads to a circular chamber about twenty feet in diameter. This arrangement occurs again and again throughout the group of hills, and this is all, this is a Marabar Cave. Having seen one such cave, having seen two, having seen three, four, fourteen, twenty-four, the visitor returns to Chandrapore uncertain whether he has had an interesting experience or a dull one or any experience at all. He finds it difficult to discuss the caves, or to keep them apart in his mind, for the pattern never varies, and no carving, not even a bees' nest or a bat, distinguishes one from another. Nothing, nothing attaches to them, and their reputation - for they have one - does not depend upon human speech. It is as if the surrounding plain or the passing birds have taken upon themselves to exclaim 'extraordinary', and the word has taken root in the air, and been inhaled by mankind.

from A Passage to India by E.M.Forster

21

3 Making a message

Talking about events which involve only the subject : intransitive verbs

1 (Paras. 3.9 to 3.14) Use the intransitive verbs below in an appropriate tense to complete the sentences.

arise crackle doze economize elapse shiver yawn

a In order to buy a car we . . *economized* . . . as much as possible.

b I think he's asleep. He . . . . during the lesson and I'm sure he . . . .

now.

c If any problems . . . . , let me know.

d It was so cold that we . . . . all night.

e A bonfire . . . . in one of the gardens.

f A long time . . . . since we last met.

Involving someone or something other than the subject : transitive verbs

2 (Paras. 3.15 to 3.20) Use the transitive verbs below in an appropriate tense to complete the sentences.

address build display pronounce report shock take welcome

a They . . *welcomed* . . . . . . him with open arms as if he were a member of the family.

b The event . . . . her and she . . . . it to the police.

c He . . . . a house facing the river.

d . . . . the envelope and . . . . it to the postbox.

e They . . . . the words in a very strange way.

f The shopkeeper . . . . his goods beautifully.

3 (Paras. 3.2 to 3.20) Say whether the verbs in the following sentences are transitive or intransitive.

a The water evaporated.   . . . *intransitive* . . . .

b They upset the whole atmosphere at the party.   . . . .

c That dress really suits you.   . . . .

d The company presented him with a gold watch.   . . . .

e They handled the situation very carefully.   . . . .

f They dined at 9 o'clock. . . . .

g The children pelted us with snowballs. . . . .

4 Look at the pairs of sentences below, and say which verb is transitive and which is intransitive, in each pair.

a i I drove first, and the others followed. *intransitive* . . . .

   ii They followed me but then got lost. *transitive* . . . .

b i I wanted to know if the dress would fit me. . . . .

   i It fitted and I was delighted. . . . .

c i The cameramen filmed the actors in the studio. . . . .

   ii As they filmed, I relaxed. . . . .

d i She sat down and wrote. . . . .

   ii She wrote letters to all the people she knew. . . . .

e i I went upstairs and changed. . . . .

   ii I changed my trousers and my shirt. . . . .

5 (Paras. 3.2 to 3.5) Look at the following extract and underline all the verbs. Then draw a circle around the transitive verbs.

> She inserted the key in the lock, aware as she did so of the interested glance of the greengrocer, and found herself in a narrow hall. The hall smelled of apples and loam, a strong rich tank which, she guessed, overlaid less agreeable smells. It was very narrow - too narrow for a pram, she told herself - and obstructed by two sacks of potatoes and a meshed bag of onions. To the right an open door led into the shop; a second, with a glass panel, gave sight of a back yard.

from Innocent Blood by P.D.James

6 (Para. 3.21) Make two sentences with each of the openings on the left by choosing suitable adjuncts of place from the right.

i The police escorted the man	**a**	on the mantlepiece.
ii We treated her	**b**	with great care.
iii He positioned the ornaments	**c**	away.
iv They led the dog	**d**	as kindly as possible.
	e	to everything she wanted.
	f	out of the room.

i	ii	iii	iv
c			
f			

7 (Para. 3.22) Use one of the verbs from paragraph 3.22 in an appropriate tense to complete each gap below.

a A car slowed down as it . . . . .*approached*. . . . . . . the traffic lights.

b We . . . . the wood and saw some deer which . . . . it.

c They . . . . neighbouring offices at work.

d I didn't recognise the town at first. Then, as we . . . . the corner of Elms Avenue, and

. . . . the house where I was born, I realised I was on familiar ground.

e Enthusiastic crowds . . . . the streets.

Verbs where the object refers back to the subject : reflexive verbs

8 (Paras. 3.27 to 3.32) Use the list in paragraph 3.29 to fill in the blanks in the following exercise. You need to add a verb and a reflexive pronoun.

a I . . . .*enjoy*. . . . .*myself*. . . . . . . immensely when I'm doing this kind of work.

b He got the children ready and then went to . . . .

c We enjoyed the holiday but found it difficult to . . . . to the humidity.

d She thinks clearly, but finds it difficult to . . . . effectively.

Verbs with little meaning : delexical verbs

9 (Para. 3.34) Use a delexical verb to fill each gap, and then choose the most appropriate phrase from the right hand column to complete each sentence.

i	He's . . . .*made*. . . a confession	**a**	that she has kept.
ii	You should . . . . respect	**b**	not to forget again.
iii	They're . . . . an attempt	**c**	at last - now we know who did it.
iv	I've . . . . the decision	**d**	when you cross the road.
v	They've . . . . an enquiry	**e**	to do it immediately.
vi	I've . . . . the suggestion	**f**	for other people's property.
vii	She's . . . . the blame	**g**	to put things right.
viii	He . . . . me a warning	**h**	into what happened.
ix	Please . . . . care	**i**	although I think someone else did it.
x	She . . . . a promise	**j**	that we could go out tonight.

i	ii	iii	iv	v	vi	vii	viii	ix	x
c									

10 (Paras. 3.49 to 3.50) Choose verbs from the list in paragraph 3.49 to complete the sentences below. You need to use each verb twice, once transitively and once intransitively.

a i My jacket . . . . . *is hanging* . . . . over there - can't you see it?

ii The revolutionaries . . . . . . *hanged* . . . . . . the man they suspected of being a spy.

b i The children . . . . when we played cards.

ii A swindler . . . . him of what was supposed to be his.

c i They had a race, and he . . . .

ii He . . . . third prize in the race.

d i I was watching TV while you . . . .

ii I . . . . her face to she if she was telling the truth.

e i It was the first time he . . . .

ii It was the first time he . . . . a bus.

f i We . . . . for more pay.

ii The young man . . . . his father in his rage.

Now write similar pairs of sentences, choosing other verbs from the list in paragraph 3.49.

. . . .

. . . .

. . . .

. . . .

. . . .

Verbs which can be used in both intransitive and transitive clauses

11 (Para. 3.53) Decide which of the objects underlined you could omit in the text below without making the meaning unclear. Circle them.

We had quite an adventure yesterday. Tim and I had forgotten the key to the house and couldn't enter the door. We knew Chris was asleep inside but he couldn't hear the knocking. We asked a neighbour for help but he explained that he didn't have a spare key. We telephoned the house to try and talk to Chris. He was fast asleep, so five minutes later we phoned Chris again, but with no luck! So we had to try other methods of entering. We tried pushing the door; we pushed it and pushed it - but no luck! Then we thought about other possibilities. We considered these possibilities carefully and decided to sing a song together. We began a song and passers-by joined in the song. It sounded terrible! But it worked! Chris heard us and opened the door. We've learned a lesson - we'll always remember our keys in future!

Changing your focus by changing the subject : ergative verbs

12 (Paras. 3.60 to 3.68) Complete each sentence opening on the left with a verb on the right.

i	The gymnast balanced, then her body	a	shattered.
ii	He added flour and the sauce	b	improved a lot.
iii	After the illness, she looked older - she had really	c	defrosted overnight.
iv	A burglar had entered the house and the alarm bell	d	shrank.
v	The new teacher's really good - my English has	e	reversed.
vi	They took the food out of the freezer, so it	f	rang.
vii	I used water which was too hot and my trousers	g	aged dramatically.
viii	We saw the car move forward, then it	h	roasted slowly.
ix	He threw a ball and the glass	i	thickened.
x	We put a turkey in the oven and it	j	turned gracefully.

i	ii	iii	iv	v	vi	vii	viii	ix	x
j									

13 (Paras. 3.60 to 3.68) Rewrite the following sentences.

a The latest model is very popular - we've sold a lot.

The latest model *has sold well.* . . . .

b They quickened their pace as the light began to fail.

Their pace . . . .

c She melted the butter in a saucepan.

The butter . . . .

d The waves rocked the boat gently.

The boat . . . .

Verbs which involve people doing the same thing to each other : reciprocal verbs

14 (Para. 3.71) Complete the sentences below. Be careful to add an appropriate preposition if necessary.

a I first met my penfriend last year, although we . . . . *had corresponded with* . . . . each other

since we were teenagers.

b She and her parents found it difficult . . . . with each other.

c We hadn't seen one another for a long time - so we . . . . and

. . . . each other.

d We . . . . each other because we couldn't agree which TV programme we

wanted to watch.

Verbs which can have two objects : ditransitive verbs

15 (Paras. 3.74 to 3.83) Decide whether these gaps should be filled by 'to', 'for' or
nothing at all.

a I wrote a card . . . . *to* . . . . . her and posted it . . . . her wishing . . . . her a happy

birthday and promising . . . . her a longer letter in which I would tell . . . . her our

arrival time.

b He cooked a meal . . . . the visitors and showed it . . . . his wife before serving it

. . . . them. It was wonderful food - he begrudged . . . . them nothing.

c We had promised . . . . the children that we would take them . . . . the circus, so we

bought some tickets.

Extending or changing the meaning of a verb : phrasal verbs

16 (Paras. 3.87; 3.89) Decide which of the following are true. There is more than
one correct answer in each case. Use a Cobuild dictionary if necessary.

i If you use these verbs, you are
talking about money:

    a pay up
    b rattle through
    c club together
    d tamper with
    e settle up
    f splash out
    g shop around

ii If you use these verbs, you are talking about
food or drink:

    a opt out
    b dine out
    c drink to
    d dispose of
    e boil over
    f stock up
    g romp through

iii If you use these verbs, you are talking about
sleep or rest:

    a butt in
    b doze off
    c sit down
    d lie in
    e sit back
    f lash out
    g flake out

17 (Paras. 3.93 to 3.95) Using a Cobuild dictionary if necessary, try to find one phrasal verb in each group which is inappropriate.

a

| do up |
| take on | a flat |
| pack off |
| board up |

b

| scale down |
| smooth over |
| think over | a problem |
| weed out |
| sort out |
| hush up |

c

| rub out |
| colour in |
| cross out |
| pin up | a picture |
| piece together |
| tear up |
| doll up |

d

| draw up |
| rush through |
| rule out |
| thrash out | an agreement |
| frighten away |
| hammer out |

e

| soak up |
| top up |
| wipe up | a liquid |
| wipe away |
| hammer out |

f

| bail out |
| hunt down |
| fight off |
| shoot down | a criminal |
| track down |
| smooth over |

g

| fill in |
| fill up |
| shoot down | a form |
| tear up |
| tidy away |

h

| frighten away |
| warn off |
| throw out | an intruder |
| fight off |
| add up |

18 (Paras. 3.95 to 3.97) Decide which phrasal verb can be used in each of the following pairs of sentences.

a A plane . . . . *took* . . . . . *off* . . . . . .

Moira . . . . . *took* . . . . . *off* . . . . . her coat.

b They felt very seasick and

. . . .

He . . . . the ball . . . . into the air.

c We . . . . very early on

our journey.

We . . . . the problem . . . . as clearly as possible.

d He was sitting quite still, then he

. . . .

He . . . . the words . . . . in the dictionary.

19 (Para. 3.99) Rewrite the following sentences, using ergative phrasal verbs.

a He woke her up.   She . . . . *woke up.* . . . .

b He wakes his wife up at 8am.   His wife . . . .

c They have closed down the old cinema.   The old cinema . . . .

d They will check passengers in at 1.30.   Passengers . . . .

20 (Para. 3.106) Complete the following sentences. Add an appropriate personal pronoun in each case.

a He's very rude to her - he always. . . . . *answers her back.* . . . .

b Our twins are so alike that you can't . . . .

c She didn't want to go along with them but in the end they . . . .

d The neighbours were waiting outside so I . . . .

21 (Para 3.113) Choose the most appropriate verb on the right to follow each sentence opening on the left. Add an appropriate pronoun in the blanks.

i	He had a good relationship with her - he	**a**	went through with . . . .
ii	It's no wonder they don't like him - he has always	**b**	talked down to . . . .
iii	We had planned to emigrate for ages and although we were nervous we	**c**	got on with . . . *her.* . . . .
iv	He always managed to avoid doing a job - he	**d**	looked up to . . . .
v	I didn't feel like working but eventually I	**e**	kept up with . . . .
vi	She's much younger than her brother, but during the walk she	**f**	wriggled out of . . . .
vii	They don't get on with their father but when they were small they	**g**	caught up with . . . .
viii	She was ill, so she was behind the rest of the class, but she soon	**h**	got down to . . . .

i	ii	iii	iv	v	vi	vii	viii
c							

Verbs which consist of two parts : compound verbs

22 (Paras. 3.123 to 3.125) Decide what each verb on the left refers to, choosing one phrase from the list on the right.

a	You **double-glaze**	**i**	a person, when you trick them.
b	You **double-cross**	**ii**	a window with two sheets of glass.
c	You **double-check**	**iii**	a car alongside another car.
d	You **double-park**	**iv**	something you're not sure about.
e	If you **cross-check** something, you	**v**	ask someone a lot of detailed questions.
f	If you **cross-examine** someone, you	**vi**	write a note in a book to refer to another section of the book.
g	If you **cross-question** someone, you	**vii**	look at data from a different point of view to check it.
h	If you **cross-reference something**, you	**viii**	ask a lot of questions.

Noun groups as complements of link verbs

23 (Para. 3.148) Complete the gaps in the following sentences with link verbs.

a She ...._had grown into_........ one of the most beautiful young women I had ever seen.

b What the problem .... was far less than we had expected.

c It's now .... a far more serious state of affairs.

d I immediately .... her for advice.

Describing the object of a verb : object complements

24 (Para. 3.170) Fill in the gaps in the following sentences with verbs from the list in paragraph 3.170.

a The doctor ......_certified_................. him dead.

b I .... Catherine, but my friends call me Katy.

c The area .... a national monument.

d William .... 'Billy'.

e They .... him insane, although he wasn't.

Indicating what role something has or how it is perceived : the preposition 'as'

25 (Para. 3.181) Complete the sentence openings on the left with appropriate endings on the right.

i	The people in the village have branded him	**a**	as a traitor.
ii	During the war she was denounced	**b**	as a thief.
iii	The censors certified the film	**c**	as the 60th President.
iv	I only intended that	**d**	as having long dark hair.
v	The nation elected him	**e**	as a joke.
vi	He described her	**f**	as being unsuitable for children.

i	ii	iii	iv	v	vi
_b_					

Talking about two actions done by the same person : phase verbs together

26 (Paras. 3.190 to 3.195) Decide which sentence is correct in each of the pairs below.

a "I'll go to the USA this summer" she said.
   i She wants to go to the USA.
   ii She wants going to the USA.

b "I'll help you" he promised.
   i He means to help us.
   ii He means helping us.

c "I should pass the exam" she said.
   i She expects passing the exam.
   ii She expects to pass the exam.

d "I might buy a dog" he said.
   i He's considering to buy a dog.
   ii He's considering buying a dog.

e "I'm going to get a better job" she said.
   i She's resolved to get a better job.
   ii She's resolved getting a better job.

f "I'll come with you" her mother said.
   i Her mother's promised going with her.
   ii Her mother's promised to go with her.

Talking about two actions done by different people : phase verbs separated by an object

27 (Paras. 3.205 to 3.207) Complete the gaps in the following sentences. Choose an appropriate verb from the lists in paragraphs 3.205 and 3.207 and then add one of the verbs in the box given below. You need to decide whether the second verb should be a present participle or a 'to' – infinitive.

develop do obey play read sing take wait

a She's very good at . . . *listening to* . . . . the children . . . *reading* . . . . . .

b I . . . . our cat . . . . with her kittens.

c The students sometimes . . . . their teachers . . . . all their work for them!

d After a long time I . . . . my brother . . . . me for a meal, at a local restaurant.

e She got stuck in a traffic jam on the way to the dentist's and I'm afraid she . . . . him . . . . half an hour.

f I . . . . him . . . . in the bath - it did sound funny!

g Their parents . . . . them . . . . their talents in music and art.

h The sergeant . . . . the soldiers . . . . every command.

4 Varying the message

Statements, questions, orders, and suggestions

1 (Para. 4.2) Write down the function of each of these sentences. Choose from the functions below.

give information   obtain information   express an opinion   give an order   make a promise   make a suggestion

a I've lived here for a number of years. ..... *give information*

b Why did you do that? .....

c That's exactly what I think. .....

d If I were you, I'd ask him myself. .....

e I'll write to you as soon as I can. .....

f Sit down and listen to us. .....

g It's on the corner by the traffic lights. .....

h Could you tell me what this says? .....

i Why don't you lie down and try to sleep? .....

j It's time you left. .....

k I'll do whatever you say. .....

l It's not as tasty as I'd hoped it would be. .....

2 (Para. 4.4) Underline the main verbs and the subjects, if they are given, and say what mood is used.

a <u>I'd like</u> to know how you feel. ..... *declarative*

b Write down the answer immediately. .....

c Have you taken it all in? .....

d Speak up, please. .....

e He jotted down some notes on a pad. .....

f Do it as soon as you can. .....

g He'll pop round in a minute. .....

h What exactly did you think? .....

Asking questions : the interrogative mood

3 (Paras. 4.10 to 4.11) Decide which two responses in the right hand column are most appropriate for each of the questions on the left.

i	Do you smoke?	a	Several times.
		b	Occasionally.
ii	Why didn't you come on time?	c	Yes, I can.
		d	I told him to.

iii	Has your husband ever been to Paris?	e	Exactly what you told him to do.
		f	Yes, I do.
iv	Who told you?	g	Nowhere.
		h	I hope so.
v	Are you all going away this year?	i	He did.
		j	Yes, he has.
vi	When did it happen?	k	Because I was busy.
		l	Fred.
vii	Is he listening?	m	In 1989.
		n	His homework.
viii	What's he done?	o	No, he isn't.
		p	I think it happened last year.
ix	Where's he living at the moment?	q	Not very well.
		r	Yes, we are.
x	Can you swim?	s	He's not living anywhere.
		t	I couldn't.

i	ii	iii	iv	v	vi	vii	viii	ix	x
f									
b									

'Yes/no' - questions

4 (Paras. 4.12 to 4.16) Make 'yes/no' questions. Then choose the most appropriate answer from the column on the right.

i   they/American?   *Are they American?*   a   Yes - for years.

ii   live/they/in London/ a long time?   b   Several times a year.

iii   they/have/many children?   c   Yes - they have four.

iv   be/their eldest child/a boy - a girl?   d   I expect so - they usually do.

v   they/often/go to the States?   e   Yes, they are.

vi   they/plan/to New York/this year?   f   It's a boy.

i	ii	iii	iv	v	vi
e					

'Wh'- questions

5 (Paras. 4.18 to 4.30) Read the statements below and then use 'wh' - words to write questions. Write down whether the question word refers to the subject or the object of the verb.

a I was invited to the cinema last night.

 i *Who invited you to the cinema last night? S*

 ii *Who was invited to the cinema last night? O*

b My car's in the car park.

 i ....

 ii ....

c She read the whole book.

 i ....

 ii ....

d He's writing another novel.

 i ....

 ii ....

Telling someone to do something : the imperative mood

6 (Para. 4.34) Fill in the gaps in the following sentences.

 a ...*Compare*...... this graph with the other and tell me what you think.

 b .... that I help you - will you do it then?

 c .... all the pros and cons and then decide.

 d .... you were on a desert island - what would you take with you?

 e .... yourself relaxing by the river on a sunny day.

 f .... the light colour of the ceiling with a darker colour on the walls.

 g .... the idea that she gave you and try to develop it.

Review : mood

7 Read this extract and underline the statements. Circle the questions.

'It's a beautiful thing, the destruction of words. Of course the great wastage is in the verbs and adjectives, but there are hundreds of nouns that can be got rid of as well. It isn't only the synonyms; there are also the antonyms. After all, what justification is there for a word which is simply the opposite of some other word? A word contains its opposite in itself. Take "good", for instance. If you have a word like "good", what need is there for a word like "bad"? "Ungood" will do just as well - better, because it's an exact opposite, which the other is not. Or again, if you want a stronger version of "good", what sense is there in having a whole string of vague useless words like "excellent" and "splendid" and all the rest of them? "Plusgood" covers the meaning; or "doubleplusgood" if you want something stronger still. Of course we use those forms already, but in the final version of Newspeak there'll be nothing else. In the end the whole notion of goodness and badness will be covered by only six words - in reality only one word. Don't you see the beauty of that, Winston? It was B.B.'s idea originally, of course' he added as an afterthought.

from 1984 by George Orwell

Negation : forming negative statements

8 (Para. 4.43) Fill in the gaps below using negative words.

a .... *Neither* ..... my mother .... *nor* .... my father eats fish.

b I'll .... forget my holiday in Turkey - there's .... on earth like the

coast there!

c .... can say you didn't try.

d .... of us understood the play.

e There's .... cheese left, I'm afraid.

9 (Para. 4.54) Rewrite each of these sentences using a verb from paragraph 4.54 with 'not', and a 'to' – infinitive.

a I'd like to eat early.

I don't want to eat late. ....

b He probably won't come, in my opinion.

....

c We may not go on holiday this year.

....

d I haven't got your full address.

....

10 (Paras. 4.57 to 4.75) Use the words below to complete the sentences. You can use words more than once if necessary.

neither   never   none of   not altogether   not very   nothing but   nowhere

a .... *None of* ..... them did as they were told.

b I .... would have known unless you'd told me.

c There's .... she hasn't been.

d She's .... sure that it's the best thing to do.

e .... drink and drive.

f There's .... bread in the kitchen, and I don't really want to eat bread.

g .... party was to blame.

Forming negative statements : negative affixes

11 (Paras. 4.76 to 4.80) Use prefixes to form the opposite of the following nouns.

a	..... *in* ..... ability	k	.... accuracy
b	.... practice	l	.... espionage
c	.... action	m	.... wife
d	.... information	n	.... happiness
e	.... responsibility	o	.... management
f	.... co-operation	p	.... sincerity
g	.... matter	q	.... hero
h	.... efficiency	r	.... possibility
i	.... legibility	s	.... Prime Minister
j	.... reverence	t	.... apartheid

12 (Paras. 4.76 to 4.80) Use prefixes to form the opposite of these adjectives and adverbs.

a	.... *im* mobile	k	.... courteously
b	.... aware	l	.... reliable
c	.... explicably	m	.... practical
d	.... reverent	n	.... legal
e	.... adjusted	o	.... rational
f	.... revolutionary	p	.... agreeable
g	.... clockwise	q	.... profit-making
h	.... moral	r	.... replaceable
i	.... existent	s	.... natural
j	.... productive	t	.... remarkable

13 (Paras. 4.76 to 4.80) Use prefixes to make these verbs negative.

a	.... *un* do	k	.... code
b	.... fuse	l	.... attack
c	.... connect	m	.... lead
d	.... inform	n	.... classify
e	.... tie	o	.... sensitize
f	.... approve	p	.... obey
g	.... lay	q	.... construe
h	.... calculate	r	.... escalate
i	.... stick	s	.... read
j	.... treat	t	.... agree

14 (Para. 4.81) Decide which negative adjectives in the right hand column are most appropriate to complete the sentence openings on the left.

i	Their house burned down and ever since they have been	a	worthless.
ii	I couldn't understand his reaction - it was	b	speechless.
iii	Don't bother to keep those old coins - they're	c	harmless.
iv	Throw away that old machine - it's	d	restless.
v	When I finished the run I was quite	e	homeless.
vi	The flowers you gave me are lovely - I'm absolutely	f	breathless.
vii	He slept very badly - he was really	g	useless.
viii	Don't worry about the dog - he's	h	meaningless.

i	ii	iii	iv	v	vi	vii	viii
e							

15 (Para. 4.82) Complete the sentences below, using the words in brackets.

a Our car has been stolen. **(car)**

We are . . . . *carless* . . . .

b He's a refugee. **(state)**

He's . . . .

c We've got no money. **(penny)**

We're . . . .

d The tree hasn't got any leaves on it. **(leaf)**

It's . . . .

e He's unemployed at present. **(job)**

He's . . . .

f There are no clouds in the sky. **(cloud)**

It's . . . .

Now write more sentences, adding '-less' to other nouns to describe a lack of something.

Forming negative statements : broad negatives

16 (Para. 4.83) Use broad negatives to fill in the gaps below.

I . . . . *hardly* . . . . ever sunbathe - where I live the sun is . . . . hot enough and we . . . . have hot summers. We do have garden chairs, but we . . . . use them, so they are . . . . worn.

Emphasizing the negative aspect of a statement

17 (Paras. 4.91 to 4.94) Choose words to complete the sentences below.

a bit   at all   the least bit   in the slightest   whatsoever   nothing whatsoever

a He wasn't . . . . . . *the least bit* . . . . . . concerned about what you said.

b I don't miss them . . . .

c We could say . . . . to persuade him to stay.

d He did it without any help . . . . from his parents.

e He's not . . . . sorry for what he did.

f It's of no use . . . . - get rid of it.

Review : Negation

18 *Complete the following sentences.

a I hardly . . . .

b . . . . anything whatsoever.

c My teacher rarely . . . .

d . . . . in the least.

e Neither . . . .

f I've never . . . .

g Nobody . . . .

h I don't intend . . . .

Using modals

19 (Para. 4.95) Underline the modals in the following sentences, and draw a circle around the semi-modals.

a I ought to ask him, but I daren't.

b She might type it if you ask her - she used to be a secretary.

c He needs to see a specialist and should make an appointment immediately.

d Shall we leave now, or can we wait a bit longer?

Special features of modals

20 (Paras. 4.102 to 4.109) Make questions and negative statements from the following sentences.

a He'll arrive.
   Will he arrive?   He won't arrive.

b We should leave.

   . . . .

c You ought to have written.

. . . .

d They'd have told me.

. . . .

21 (Para. 4.109) Choose two appropriate responses on the right for each of the statements on the left.

i	I think it's raining.		**a**	Yes, he should.

i I think it's raining.

ii He should have worked harder.

iii I expect we'll have chicken tonight.

iv We must see that film.

a Yes, he should.

b I thought it would.

c Yes - we must see it.

d You're right - he really should have done.

e Yes - I thought it would rain.

f Yes - I suppose we will.

g Yes - we must.

h Yes - I suppose we will have it again!

i	ii	iii	iv
b			
e			

Referring to time

22 (Paras. 4.110 to 4.117) Underline each modal in the following sentences. Say whether each sentence refers to the past, the present or the future.

a He'<u>ll</u> always do what you want. . . . . *present* . . . .

b They wouldn't accept what we told them. . . . .

c She could play the piano really well when she was young. . . . .

d We shall see. . . . .

e They would often play lots of practical jokes on their teachers. . . . .

Indicating ability

23 (Paras. 4.119 to 4.122) State the function of 'can' or 'could' as used in the following sentences.

a I can hear an owl. . . . . *awareness* . . . .

b They could be really helpful when they tried. . . . .

c He can't sing - he's tone deaf! . . . .

d She could feel the breeze on her skin. . . . .

e They couldn't ski at all when they arrived. . . . .

f He can be very annoying sometimes. . . . .

Indicating likelihood

24 (Paras. 4.124 to 4.145) Say which modals would be appropriate to complete the following sentences. There may be more than one possible answer.

could	must	should
may	ought to	will
might	shall	would

a It . . . . . *might* . . . . . well be true.

b You . . . . all be familiar with what we're talking about.

c They . . . . arrive by 4 o'clock at the latest.

d It . . . . not be true in this particular case.

e There . . . . be a drought next summer.

f I . . . . give it to you as soon as I've finished.

g Don't touch his leg. It . . . . be broken.

Indicating permission

25 (Paras 4.146 to 4.149) Underline each modal and write down its function in the sentence.

a You <u>can</u> drive at 70mph on motorways.   *permission*
. . . .

b You may return books up to the date shown.
. . . .

c She can have it – I don't want it any more.
. . . .

d We could do what we wanted.
. . . .

e They may use the car provided that they're careful.
. . . .

f They could pick as many flowers as they liked.
. . . .

Indicating unacceptability

26 (Paras. 4.150 to 4.157) Say which modals would be appropriate to complete the following sentences. There may be more than one possible answer.

cannot	mustn't	shouldn't
may not	shall not	will not

a You . . . . . *mustn't* . . . . . smoke in this building.

b You . . . . really do that - it's not a good idea.

c She . . . . walk on the grass.

d Tobacco . . . . be sold to anyone under the age of 18.

e Unless you work hard, you . . . . pass the exam.

Review : indicating possibility

27(Paras. 4.118 to 4.157) Complete the following chart, marking a cross to show which modals (positive or negative) can be used to indicate which functions.

	can cannot	could could not	may may not	might might not	ought to ought not to
INDICATING ABILITY					
INDICATING LIKELIHOOD					
INDICATING PERMISSION					
INDICATING UNACCEPTABILITY					

	shall shall not	should should not	will will not	would would not	must must not
INDICATING ABILITY					
INDICATING LIKELIHOOD					
INDICATING PERMISSION					
INDICATING UNACCEPTABILITY					

Interacting with other people

28(Paras. to 4.160 to 4.226) Write sentences in different ways, using any modals which are appropriate. Then tick your most polite version.

a Ask someone if you can make a phone call.

Can I make a phone call?

Could I make a phone call?

May I make a phone call?

Might I possibly make a phone call? ✓

b Ask someone to lend you £5.00.

....

....

....

....

c Ask someone to stop smoking.

....

....

....

....

d Offer someone a cup of tea.

....

....

....

....

e Suggest going outside.

....

....

....

....

f Say that you refuse to talk about the accident.

....

....

....

....

g Say that you really want to go on holiday.

....

....

....

....

h Say that it's essential that you do it now.

....

....

....

....

Expressions used instead of modals

29 (Paras. 4.227 to 4.251) Choose which of the responses on the right are possible. There is more than one in each case.

i   Are you coming with us?

    a I'm sorry, I'm unable to join you.
    b I'm sorry, I won't be able to join you.
    c It's impossible for me to join you.
    d I could be able to, but I'm not sure.
    e I can be able to, but I'm not sure.
    f I might be able to, but I'm not sure.

ii   Will the post arrive soon?

    a I hope so - It has to.
    b It's got to arrive soon.
    c It's got to arrive in a minute.
    d The postman's bound to arrive soon.
    e It used to arrive soon.
    f It would arrive soon.

iii What is your brother going to do when he has finished university?

    a He intends to be a swimmer.
    b He can be able to get any job he wants.
    c He's determined to be a lawyer.
    d He's resolved to be a lawyer.
    e He got to decide for himself.
    f He doesn't intend to do anything at the moment.

Semi-modals

30 (Paras. 4.258 to 4.262) Choose endings for each of the sentence openings on the left. Add the positive or the negative form of 'used to' to each sentence.

i   There ... *used to* ..... be

    a a 'Bobby'.

ii   Australians .... have

    b an American state, now it is.

iii The British pound .... have

    c as changeable as it is now.

iv   Smoking .... be

    d pounds, shillings and pence, but now have dollars.

v   Some people would say the world climate
    ....

    e much bigger than it is now.

vi   A British Policeman .... called

    f a wall between East and West Berlin.

vii The world's equatorial rain forest
    .... be

    g considered dangerous.

viii Alaska .... be

    h 100 pence, but now it has.

i	ii	iii	iv	v	vi	vii	viii
f							

5 Expressing time

The present in general : the simple present

1 (Paras. 5.8 to 5.16) Find pairs of examples in which the simple present is used in the same situation or for the same reason. Say what that situation or reason is.

i	I **promise** that it's true.	a	She seldom **scrubs** the doorstep.
ii	A sperm **fertilises** the egg.	b	Romeo **walks** across the stage and **sees** Juliet.
iii	We **live** in a suburb of London.	c	I **admit** that this is a bit late.
iv	He **kicks** the ball to Smith.	d	She **plays** the star role.
v	I **hear** you got the job.	e	They **tell** me you've been ill.
vi	He **commutes** daily.	f	He**'s** an eminent surgeon.
vii	He **portrays** a sad character.	g	Metal **expands** and **contracts**.

i	ii	iii	iv	v	vi	vii
c						

2 Complete these sentences, using one of the following verbs in the simple present. Use each verb once only.

confess   earn   ebb   enclose   flow   perform   play

a Surgeons ... *perform* ...... operations and usually .... very high salaries.

b He .... the villain in the film.

c The tide .... and ....

d I .... that I completely forgot your birthday.

e I .... my application form and c.v.

Accent on the present : present continuous

3 (Paras. 5.17 to 5.20; 5.24) Find pairs of sentences where the present continuous is used in the same situation or for the same reason. Say what that situation or reason is.

i	I**'m doing** these exercises.	a	The children **are getting** more exercise now they're at school.
ii	My husband**'s learning** to drive this year.	b	London's skyline **is changing**.
iii	We**'re eating** healthier food than before.	c	The children **are** forever **knocking** over their drinks.
iv	You**'re** always **borrowing** my things.	d	She**'s using** my pen.
v	The value of the pound **is** gradually **falling**.	e	I**'m working** from home at the moment.

i	ii	iii	iv	v
d				

Emphasizing time in the present : using adjuncts

4 (Paras. 5.21 to 5.25) * Complete the following sentences.

a Nowadays people . . . .

b In my country we traditionally . . . .

c I usually . . . .

d These days young people . . . .

e My best friend is always . . . .

f In this day and age . . . .

Review : The present

5 Complete each gap with a verb in either the simple present or the present continuous.

Dear Erica,

We . . . . . *are enjoying* . . . . . . our holiday a lot. Each day we . . . . the usual things –

we . . . . down to the beach, ... a dip in the sea,

. . . . in the sun for a while – that's what we . . . . at the moment –

although Eddie . . . . to annoy me – he . . . . cold water over my

back while I . . . . this letter.

We . . . . both really tanned and I . . . . very healthy. We

. . . . to windsurf – it . . . . much easier than I thought.

We . . . . you were here.

Love from Janet

6 Underline all the verbs in the simple present and put a circle round all the verbs in the present continuous.

The Little Calf is now eight months old. A human child at this age is trying to lift its body from the floor, to cling briefly to chairs, and to reach for the hem of mother's skirt. The Little Calf, by contrast, is well along the road to independence; if his mother were to disappear overnight he might perhaps survive alone.

The Little Calf and his mother are feeding 400 miles at sea off San Francisco. They will go no farther north this year, though many of their companions have dropped from sight over the horizon, far on their way to the Bering Sea. The females that came into heat have dallied behind. The pattern of the herd as the Little Calf knew it in spring is dissolving. Whales of like age and sex and breeding disposition are now consorting; the groups are separating in space because of the differences in their swimming speeds.

The day is mild. A filmy diffusion pales the blue of the sky and gives a soft extra light. A gentle breeze touches the moving sea. Here and there the surface breaks in a pattern of light, struck by a shower of needles. Schools of sauries, each holding a million fish, break and boil to the top. Their sides are gleaming iridescent silver; their backs are metallic blue-green. The Little Calf and his mother, along with seven other females, the harem bull, and a young male, are lazily following the fish, feasting as they go. During the bright of day, when the schools descend for reasons of their own - reasons unknown to man - the old whales pursue them down, during the night the young whales plunge with open jaws through the silver masses. Even the Little Calf, though nursing, is swallowing the fat, tasty, ten-inch fish.

from The Year of the Whale by Victor B.Scheffer

Stating a definite time in the past : the simple past

7 (Paras. 5.27 to 5.30) Use one of the following verbs in the simple past to fill in the gaps in these newspaper extracts. You can use a verb more than once if necessary.

affect attack avert be cling die do drink drive off fall leave put out report say try use vote

a
PG Chimp Dies

Joey the chimpanzee, one of the earliest stars of the PG Tips tea advertisement, ...*died*........of a heart attack aged 39. Brian Le Grys, owner of Suffolk Wildlife Park, ... Joey .... a cup of tea just before he ....

from The Independent on Sunday

b
Soccer Fire

Police ....disaster at Bristol City's football ground when they ....a fire under a stand containing 300 people just after the kick-off of an FA cup tie between Bristol City and Cambridge United.

from The Independent on Sunday

c

Digital tip-off

A burglar who . . . . to take a safe from a business in Greater Manchester . . . . two clues – his fingertips. Detectives . . . . the safe . . . . on his hands.

from The Independent on Sunday

d

Vote for Freedom

Namibia's constitution assembly . . . . unanimously to declare independence from South Africa at midnight on March 21, the South African Press Association . . . .

e

Rottweilers Flee PC's Truncheon

A policeman . . . . his truncheon to save a girl who . . . . knocked to the ground by two rottweilers which . . . . her spaniel. Diane Aldridge, 16, ... to her dog as PC Chris Aldridge, 27, ... the eight-stone dogs in Shoebury, Essex.

f

The Guardian

We apologise to those readers who . . . . not receive the Guardian on Saturday when mechanical problems at our London printing plant . . . . some later editions.

from The Guardian

Accent on the past : the past continuous

8 (Paras. 5.27 to 5.32) Use these verbs to complete the gaps below, using the past continuous or the past simple where appropriate.

fall feel fracture go lose present slip

A small girl ....*fell*.............. off the stage at Sunningbury Junior School last Friday and seriously .... her leg. She .... a bouquet of flowers to the headmistress at the time, but she .... her footing and ....
She .... straight into hospital and her parents say that yesterday she .... much better.

The past in relation to the present : the present perfect

9 Use these verbs to fill the gaps in the extracts below, using the present perfect or the simple past, as appropriate.

be have jackknife say spill tell undermine use vow

a   Global warming and pollution *have undermined* the 100 year old Koppens system of climatic classification which the foreign office .... to calculate allowances for such necessities as pith helmets and bottled water.

b   A tug-of-love mum .... to continue her battle to win back custody of her children. Speaking from Cairo, Egypt, the mother .... she .... devastated by an Egyptian court ruling that her three children must stay with their Egyptian father.

c   A lorry .... on the M1 last night and its contents .... over the northbound carriage. Several lorries .... similar accidents this month in the same place and experts are to inspect the site this morning.

Events before a particular time in the past : the past perfect

10 (Paras. 5.37 to 5.39) Choose the sentence on the right which best follows each sentence on the left.

i	The plane took off at 11.	a	We were furious - if only we hadn't overslept.
ii	The plane was taking off.	b	It was a lovely flight.
iii	The plane had taken off.	c	It was so frustrating - we could actually see the plane!

Emphasizing time in the past : using adjuncts

11 (Paras. 5.40 to 5.51) Choose time adjuncts from the list below to complete the gaps.

ago   all day   ever since   this morning   yesterday evening

a We've lived in the same house . . . . *ever since* . . . . 1924.

b Two weeks . . . . they went on holiday to the same place as they had visited the year

   before.

c He was supposed to deliver the newspaper . . . . but he came

   . . . . instead.

d It had been snowing hard . . . . but it finally stopped at around

   6 o'clock.

Review : the past

12 (Paras. 5.26 to 5.51) Say which past tense has been used, and why, in the following sentences.

a I was forever tidying up after everyone else.
   past continuous – repeated actions
. . . .

b He had had piano lessons until he was 15.

. . . .

c There have been several thefts this month.

. . . .

d She contacted her parents every week.

. . . .

e We've lived here since the early '70s.

. . . .

f They'd hoped that their daughter would come home.

. . . .

13 *Complete each sentence below, using a suitable past tense.

a . . . . since the beginning of this year.

b Recently I . . . .

c . . . . the day before yesterday.

d This morning I . . . .

e . . . . for two years.

f Six months ago I . . . .

The future

14 (Paras. 5.53 to 5.65) Say which tense is used to indicate the future in each of the following sentences.

a We'll do it as soon as possible.   . . . . *modal 'will'* . . . .

b She's going to have a break.   . . . .

c They'll be arriving shortly.   . . . .

d People will usually do what they want in the end.   . . . .

e He's due to make up his mind by tomorrow.   . . . .

f I'll have been living here for 20 years in March.   . . . .

g Our flight takes off at 8.35.   . . . .

h We're arriving by train.   . . . .

15 (Paras. 5.60 to 5.62) Choose the most appropriate adjuncts on the left to link with the future events on the right.

i	Some day	**a**	I'll be more careful.
ii	One of these days	**b**	I'll get round to tidying my room.
iii	In the future	**c**	you'll have an accident unless you're more careful.
iv	Sooner or later	**d**	they'll find out where she is.
v	In future	**e**	people will have to be more aware of the environment.

i	ii	iii	iv	v
b				

Timing by adjuncts

16 (Para. 5.70) Choose suitable adjuncts from the first part of the list in paragraph 5.70 to fill in the gaps below.

a I called the doctor, and he arrived . . . . *at once.* . . . . .

b I called the doctor, and he . . . . came round.

c I waited for the doctor all morning. . . . . he arrived.

d I phoned the doctor, who said he'd come round . . . .

17 (Paras. 5.75 to 5.83) * Complete the following sentences.

   a Up till now,. . . . .

   b I'm still. . . . .

   c I . . . . yet.

   d I am no longer. . . . .

Time expressions and prepositional phrases

18 (Paras. 5.84 to 5.85) Decide which of the following responses are possible.
There is more than one correct answer in each case.

i	What time do you get up?	**a**	At 8.15.
		b	At fifteen past 8.
		c	At quarter past 8.
		d	At a quarter past 8.
		e	At eight fifteen.
		f	At eight and a quarter.
ii	When is the news on?	**a**	At ten to six.
		b	At a fifth to six.
		c	At 5.50.
		d	At fifty minutes past five.
		e	At five fifty.
		f	At ten minutes to six.
iii	What time is his plane scheduled to take off?	**a**	At 13.00.
		b	At 1 o'clock pm.
		c	At 1pm.
		d	At 13.00 pm.
		e	At one o'clock.
		f	At one.

19 (Paras. 5.90 to 5.99) Put one of the following prepositions in each gap.

at by during in on over

   a He had planned to take the exam . . . . . *in* . . . . . September but in fact he took it . . . . the beginning of October and only got the results . . . . the New Year.

   b . . . . the lecture he didn't appear to be listening, but . . . . the end he asked some very relevant questions.

   c He was very ill . . . . June, but got better . . . . the summer. . . . . the end of August, ... the 30th August to be exact, he went back to work.

   d She'd already learned to swim . . . . the time she was four.

   e . . . . the Seventies, fashions changed considerably, and they changed just as much again . . . . the following decade.

Frequency and duration

20(Para. 5.113) Choose units of time to complete the sentences below.

  a A minute is sixty . . . *seconds* . . . . . .

  b There are ten . . . . in a . . . .

  c We are living in the twentieth . . . .

  d There are twelve . . . . in a . . . .

  e People usually work during the . . . . , not at . . . .

  f There are sixty . . . . in an . . . .

21(Para. 5.114) Complete the following sentences with suitable adverbs or adverbial expressions.

  a She had the pain . . . . . *sporadically* . . . . . . at first, but when she had it . . . .

  she went to the doctor.

  b He . . . . does any work, but he . . . . gets good results.

  c I . . . . do the gardening, so there are lots of weeds.

  d I don't often go swimming, but I do . . . .

  e I haven't . . . . been to the USA, but I . . . . meet

  Americans in my job.

22(Para. 5.120) Choose the adverbs on the right which are most appropriate for the events on the left.

i	The clock chimes	**a**	yearly.
ii	Our post is delivered	**b**	monthly.
iii	I get paid	**c**	hourly.
iv	We settle our gas bill	**d**	quarterly.
v	They fill in a tax form	**e**	daily.

23(Para. 5.124) Use the prepositions in paragraph 5.124 to complete the following text.

The building of the Tower of London was started . . . . *in* . . . . . 1067, ... the Norman Conquest, and went on . . . . a number of centuries. Buildings were added . . . . the 12th Century, and the Tower as you will see it today was not completed . . . . later.

It is only . . . . the Tower opened to tourists that it has become Britain's number one tourist attraction with thousands of visitors going through the turnstiles a year. Once inside, they are willing to queue up . . . . a second time - sometimes . . . . an hour or so, to see the Crown Jewels, which are housed in the Tower.

6 Expressing manner and place

Position of adjuncts

1 (Paras. 6.7 to 6.15) Place the adjuncts (given in brackets) in the appropriate places in the sentences below.

a He's absent-minded. (somewhat)

He's somewhat absent-minded.
....

b She's well-known. (for her generosity)

....

c These scissors are useless. (simply)

....

d The house is kept clean. (meticulously, normally)

....

e He speaks to the children. (really, loudly)

....

f They remembered what they had been told. (quickly)

....

g The children are very helpful. (in their own way, usually)

....

h He forgets to do his homework. (frequently, on time)

....

Adverb forms and meanings related to adjectives

2 (Para. 6.21) Complete the sentences below with suitable adverbs from the list in paragraph 6.21.

a There are . . . . *hardly* . . . . . any people out today - it's really cold.

b She's . . . . wearing any clothes.

c I'm coming along . . . .

d I haven't felt too good . . . .

e The post should arrive . . . .

3 (Para. 6.26) Complete the gaps in the following pairs of sentences with suitable adverbs from the list in paragraph 6.26. In each pair the adverbs have different meanings.

a i The sea was . . . . *clear* . . . . . and cold.

  ii I could see him . . . . *clearly* . . . . . .

b i The flight went . . . . from London to Edinburgh.

ii The sun was almost . . . . overhead.

c i He came . . . . in the competition.

ii He came to visit us . . . . , then went home.

d i He passed the exam . . . .

ii The exam wasn't . . . .

e i The company was . . . . in debt.

ii It was . . . . satisfying.

Comparative and superlative adverbs

4 (Paras. 6.30 to 6.35) Choose the responses which are possible. There is more than one response in each case.

i You're looking fit! Have you done a lot of running recently?

    a I'm training much more harder.
    b I'm training much harder.
    c I can run much quicker now.
    d Yes - I can run much more quickly now.
    e Yes - I'm fastest in my club.
    f Yes - I run the fastest in my club.

ii Do you train with the same team?

    a Yes - we're doing better than before.
    b I'm relying on it more and more heavily for support.
    c Yes - our speed is improving more quickly than before.
    d Yes - we're getting better - but we're working much harder.
    e Yes - we're training much more hard.
    f Yes - we're hardly training.

Adverbs of manner

5 (Para. 6.40) Choose an adverb in the right hand column to complete each sentence.

i I loved the part of the film where he kissed her   a bitterly.

ii It was an easy task, but he did it very   b reluctantly.

iii She'd never tried before, but she went on stage quite   c proudly.

iv They'd had bad experiences and spoke very   d passionately.

v He's a very friendly person and always greets us   e confidently.

vi He came in after a long day and sat down   f sincerely.

vii I do mean it   g wearily.

viii They accepted the award   h cheerfully.

i	ii	iii	iv	v	vi	vii	viii
d							

6 (Paras. 6.41 to 6.44) Complete the sentences below with suitable adverbs from the lists in paragraphs 6.41 and 6.42.

a He ...... *sincerely* .... hoped I would change my mind.

b She worked .... until the children went to school and then started working

....

c She's a brilliant boss - she knows .... when someone needs support.

d He hurled himself .... at the Prince.

e They entered the country .... but have since been naturalised

....

f She thinks very ...., so she makes a good mathematician.

g He flew .... from London to Sydney.

Adverbs of degree

7 (Paras. 6.46 to 6.52) Put the adjuncts in brackets in the correct places in the following sentences.

a I've enjoyed all the lessons. **(tremendously)**

.... *I've enjoyed all the lessons tremendously.* ....

b I've enjoyed all the lessons. **(really)**

....

c He's lost all his money. **(virtually)**

....

d You knew what I was talking about. **(perfectly, well)**

....

e I'm disgusted by her behaviour. **(positively)**

....

f He works - but he dreams. **(hard, reasonably, a great deal)**

....

Review : Adverbs

8 *Use the following adverbs to make sentences. These could be about your English studies, yourself, or people or places you know.

absolutely carefully hardly intensely somewhat very much virtually

....

....

....

....

....

. . . .

. . . .

. . . .

9 (Paras. 6.36 to 6.52 and 6.82 to 6.90) Put each of these adverbs in the appropriate place in the chart below.

abroad	beautifully	immensely	silently	utterly
almost	carefully	meticulously	somewhat	vaguely
angrily	downstairs	near	terribly	virtually
ashore	downstream	overseas	underfoot	well
badly	fiercely	profoundly	underneath	wonderfully

ADVERBS OF MANNER	ADVERBS OF DEGREE	ADVERBS OF PLACE
angrily	*almost*	*abroad*

Giving information about place : prepositions

10 (Paras. 6.53 to 6.57) Underline the prepositions in the following sentences.

a The police van drew up alongside and we all got out of the car.

b She looked up at the roof and saw the bird on the tiles.

c It's beyond the church, next to the post office.

d Among his baggage was a medicine chest.

Position of prepositional phrases

11 (Para. 6.58) Rewrite the following sentences, using one of the verbs in paragraph 6.58.

a We usually put our coats on the hooks.

Our coats usually . . . . *hang on the hooks.* . . . .

b We keep our hats and scarves in the drawer.

Our hats and scarves. . . . .

c He didn't go out of the house after his illness.

He . . . .

d At present our home is in London.

We . . . .

12(Para. 6.58) Read the following passage. Then write a similar passage about the place where you live.

London is in the south of England, and it is situated on the River Thames. About 6.7 million people live there, and in addition over a million visitors stay there every year.

. . . .

. . . .

. . . .

. . . .

. . . .

Indicating position

13(Paras. 6.64 to 6.68) This is a plan of where people sat at a dinner. Write the names of those who attended in the correct places, using the information below.

James was on Helen's left and Helen was opposite her husband Steve. Joseph was opposite Tina.

Mark sat at one end of the table and Ginny was at the other end. Steve was between Alice and Paula.

Tina was next to Mark. Ginny was between Paula and Edward. James was across the table from Alice, who was next to Joseph.

14(Para. 6.69) Match each sentence opening on the left with an appropriate ending from the right.

i	Her husband sat at her bedside,	a	admiring the yachts.
ii	We walked along the quayside,	b	sipping chilled orange juice.
iii	They lay on the poolside,	c	trying to fix the puncture.
iv	She was crouching at the roadside,	d	amazed by the size of the ships.
v	We came down the mountainside,	e	and wouldn't leave.
vi	I stood at the dockside,	f	skiing as fast as we could.
vii	The farm was on the hillside,	g	very exposed to the wind.

i	ii	iii	iv	v	vi	vii
e						

15(Para. 6.72) See how many sentences you can make from the following three columns.

The house was situated	a couple of miles	behind our party.
The children were lingering	20 metres	above the town.
The tent was pitched	half a mile	outside the town.
They were snorkelling	a few thousand feet	beyond those trees.
The plane was circling	a few metres	from the shore.

The house was situated half a mile beyond those trees.

....

....

....

....

....

....

....

....

....

Indicating direction

16(Para. 6.74) Complete these sentences with suitable prepositions from the list in paragraph 6.74.

a We poured the coffee ....*into*........ the cups.

b The children raced .... their mother.

c She watched the people get .... the train.

d They moored the boat .... the jetty.

e There are a couple of shops just .... the corner.

Other ways of giving information about place

17 (Paras. 6.87 to 6.91) Decide which of the following responses are possible.

i   What was your flight like?
    a   I didn't like it when we were flying low.
    b   I didn't like it when we were flying high up.
    c   I didn't like being higher.
    d   I felt an ache, deep in my stomach.
    e   Deep down, I felt terrified.
    f   I was glad when the airport was closer.

ii How's her visit to England been?
    a   She has been everywhere.
    b   There's nowhere she hasn't been.
    c   Nowhere has she enjoyed herself so much.
    d   Nowhere she has enjoyed herself so much.
    e   She's visited anywhere.
    f   She hasn't been anywhere.

iii Are you going away this year?
    a   We're going somewhere new.
    b   We're going somewhere abroad.
    c   We're looking for somewhere to visit.
    d   We're looking for somewhere visiting.
    e   We're going anywhere we can find.
    f   We're going anywhere we can.

18 (Para. 6.94) Choose the most appropriate words in the following sentences.

a He fell **downstairs/upstairs** with a bump.

b We're going to have a picnic **indoors/outdoors**.

c We're moving **a long way/near** my mother so that we can help her more.

d The boat sailed **ashore/to sea** so that we could lay in provisions.

e The builder went **downstairs/upstairs** to gain access to the roof.

f It started raining while they were sunbathing so they grabbed everything and ran **indoors/outdoors**.

g Traffic congestion in big cities would be far worse but for efficient **overground/underground** train networks.

19 (Paras. 6.96 to 6.99) Choose sentence endings from the right which appropriately complete the openings on the left. Add adverbs or adverbial expressions from the lists in paragraphs 6.96 to 6.99 in the gaps.

i   The skater spun . . . . *round and round* . . . .   **a**   the tunnel.
ii He paced . . . .   **b**   on the ice.
iii The skier raced . . . .   **c**   the ice at great speed.
iv She skated . . . .   **d**   waiting for the news.
v   He swam . . . .   **e**   to the finish.
vi An express train rushed . . . .   **f**   against the current.

i	ii	iii	iv	v	vi
b					

Other uses of prepositional phrases

20 (Paras. 6.108 to 6.116) Say which sentences are used for each of reasons a, b, c and d.

a	referring to time	**b**	referring to manner
c	circumstances of an action	**d**	reason or cause of an action

- **i** We're going to Australia for Christmas.

- **ii** They've managed despite their problems.

- **iii** He resigned because of a disagreement.

- **iv** They travelled everywhere by bus.

- **v** She said she had worked as a nursery teacher in the Sixties.

- **vi** She scowled and made a sign with her fist.

i	ii	iii	iv	v	vi
a					

Review : prepositions

21 *Complete these sentences.

- i New York is . . . .

- ii My friend with the short dark hair. . . . .

- iii When I'm studying, I usually sit . . . .

- iv I live . . . .

22 Underline the prepositions in the following advertisement.

4 & 5 DAY CITY BREAKS
ROME, VENICE OR FLORENCE FROM £289

We are a Specialist Tour Operator providing a personal service to Italy's most beautiful Cities.
* Return Scheduled Flights from Heathrow.
* Tours and Transfers by Private Coach.
* 3 Star Hotels, all Rooms with Private Facilities.
* Breakfast & Evening Meals Included! (Venice B&B).
* Our Experienced Couriers are based in your Hotels.
* Special National Express Coach Scheme for travel to/from UK Airport.
DATES AVAILABLE: OCTOBER 1990 TO APRIL 1991.
Our Holidays fill very quickly as places are limited!
PHONE OUR BROCHURE HOTLINE TODAY
(0858) 432123

EDWARDS & HARGREAVES LTD
(FULL ABTA MEMBER A6667)

7 Reporting what people say or think

Indicating that you are reporting : reporting verbs

1 (Para. 7.7) Suggest the most suitable reporting verb for each gap.

    a 'What did you say your name was?' she . . *inquired* . . . .

    b He . . . . 'Do as I say immediately!'

    c 'What incredible luck!' she . . . .

    d 'I'd like to begin by telling you that I'm the best swimmer in the school,' he . . . .

    e 'Do students learn English as their first foreign language in your country?' he . . . .

2 (Paras. 7.9 to 7.10) Fill in the gaps in the text below with suitable reporting verbs.

My parents had . . . . *promised* . . . . that they would buy
me a car if I passed the exam, and as I . . . .
that I would pass, I . . . . that I'd spend
the whole summer touring the West Country. I had never
. . . . that I would fail, so when I opened
the envelope and . . . . that I'd got the
lowest grade possible, I was really taken aback. I just couldn't
believe that it was true. My parents were furious and they
. . . . that I should have passed. I tried
to find an excuse; I . . . . that I'd felt
ill on the day of the exam and I . . . .
that the exam room had been noisy – but I still
. . . . that I couldn't possibly have
failed, and I . . . . the headmaster that I
. . . . that a mistake had been made. He
. . . . that I might be right, as he had
. . . . that the students' grades weren't
as good as usual. The Examining Board . . . .
that the marks were correct, but then a letter arrived in which I
. . . . that I had been right – the Board
. . . . that they had made a mistake. So to
my delight, I received my car and zoomed off on my first visit to the
West of England.

3 (Para. 7.13) Link each sentence opening in the left hand column with a suitable ending on the right.

i	I never expected	a	to go away this summer.
ii	I don't imagine	b	it would rain.
iii	I don't suppose	c	she was telling the truth.
iv	We don't plan	d	to cause any damage.
v	She didn't think	e	I would get first prize.
vi	I don't want	f	we'll be able to go away this year.
vii	He didn't believe	g	you to phone so late.
viii	They don't intend	h	it will be fine enough for a picnic.

i	ii	iii	iv	v	vi	vii	viii
b							

Reporting someone's actual words : quote structures

4 (Para. 7.16) Suggest a reporting verb from the list in paragraph 7.16 to complete each of the following sentences.

a 'Please help me - I just don't know how I'll manage if you don't,' she . . . *begged* . . . .

b 'As I was saying, the situation is quite clear… ,' she . . . .

c 'Don't ever say that to me again,' I . . . .

d 'The train on platform 5 will be calling additionally at Darlington,' the loudspeaker . . . .

e 'No one ever comes to see me,' the old man . . . .

f 'You really must go now,' he . . . .

5 (Para. 7.17) Add speakers and reporting verbs on the right to suitable quotes from the left.

i	'Aaah! a mouse!'	a	I whispered.
ii	'Erm I think erm… ,'	b	he yelled.
iii	'Ssh! Keep your voice down,'	c	I screamed.
iv	'Good morning, Mrs Jones,'	d	she shrieked.
v	'You idiot,'	e	he mumbled.
vi	'Help!'	f	they chorused.

i	ii	iii	iv	v	vi
d					

Reporting statements and thoughts

6 (Para. 7.27) Complete these sentences with suitable reporting verbs, adding pronouns where necessary.

a He .... *told me* .... that I shouldn't forget to go to the dentist.

b She .... that I would find it difficult.

c They .... that they were telling the truth.

d Her sister .... that it was a good idea.

e She .... that everything would be okay in the end.

f The company .... that our expenses would be reimbursed.

g They .... that we should fill in the forms without delay.

h The police .... that he should make a statement.

Reporting questions

7 (Paras. 7.29 to 7.35) Look at the direct questions on the left. Which of the indirect questions on the right are possible? There is more than one in each group.

i The woman said 'What's your address, John?'

   a She asked him what was his address.
   b She enquired what his address was.
   c She asked him what his address was.
   d She asked him what his address is.
   e She asked what his address was.
   f She wanted to know what his address was.

ii 'Do you agree with this business plan?' the director asked the managers.

   a He asked whether or not they agreed.
   b He asked them if they agreed.
   c He asked do you agree?
   d He asked them whether they agreed.
   e He asked whether they agreed or not.
   f He asked if they agree.

iii 'What are you doing, William?' I asked myself.

   a I wanted to know what he was doing.
   b I didn't know what he was doing.
   c I wondered what was he doing.
   d I wondered what he was doing.
   e I thought what he was doing.
   f I wondered to myself what he was doing.

Reporting orders, requests, advice and intentions

8 (Paras. 7.36 to 7.45) Rewrite these sentences in different ways, changing the meaning as little as possible.

a 'Go on, apply for the job, Anthony,' Karen said.

Karen urged ...... *Anthony to apply for the job.* ....

Karen suggested ....

Karen proposed ....

b 'Peter should go to university,' said the headmaster.

The headmaster recommended . . . .

The headmaster suggested . . . .

The headmaster advised. . . . .

c 'Please give me the latest reports, Jane,' said the boss.

The boss asked . . . .

The boss instructed . . . .

The boss requested . . . .

The boss directed. . . . .

The boss demanded . . . .

d 'I expect you to pop in when you're in the area, Jenny,' David said.

David suggested . . . .

David urged . . . .

David proposed . . . .

David expects. . . . .

Avoiding mention of the person speaking or thinking

9 (Paras. 7.64 to 7.65) Complete the following sentences, using a passive form of a suitable reporting verb with the impersonal 'It'.

a *It is guaranteed* . . . . that the watch will work for longer than 6 months.

b . . . . that there are more than 5 billion people on this planet.

c . . . . that a man will one day run a mile in 3 minutes.

d . . . . that over 2,000 people were killed in the earthquake.

e . . . . that there will be another meeting next week.

10 (Para. 7.65) * Complete these sentences, using suitable reporting verbs.

a In my country it. . . . .

b Where I live it . . . .

c In today's newspaper, it. . . . .

d It. . . . .

11 (Para. 7.65) Rewrite the sentences below as phase structures.

a It is guaranteed that the food mixer will work for a year.

The food mixer . . . . *is guaranteed to work for a year.* . . . .

b It was expected that they would arrive last week.

They. . . . .

c It has been predicted that there will be snow tonight.

Snow . . . .

d It has been reported that ten people have been injured.

Ten people. . . . .

Referring to the speaker and hearer

12 (Paras. 7.68 to 7.77) Choose a speaker, reporting verb, and hearer from the second column to report each quote from the first column. Add 'to' or 'at' as appropriate.

i	'I've lost my passport,'	**a**	he confessed . . . . us.
ii	'I've done better than you,'	**b**	they revealed . . . . all of us.
iii	'Get out of here,'	**c**	she complained . . . . us.
iv	'The truth can be explained,'	**d**	the manager hinted . . . . him.
v	'I'm afraid it was my fault,'	**e**	he announced . . . . us.
vi	'I'm not at all happy about it,'	**f**	he roared . . . . me.
vii	'You're what?'	**g**	she wailed . . . . *at* . . . . . us.
viii	'The company is closing,'	**h**	I boasted . . . . her.
ix	'There's a possibility of promotion,'	**i**	he snapped . . . . us.

i	ii	iii	iv	v	vi	vii	viii	ix
g								

Review : Reporting what people say or think

13 Underline all the reporting verbs in the following extract.

"... As for the present position, I agree with a good deal of what the Dean says. But I don't consider this is the right time to act. I know this long wait hasn't improved some of our tempers. But it won't be much longer. Speaking as a fellow, I don't see any alternative to waiting. I didn't quite understand the Dean's suggestion. I do not know whether he thinks that other names ought to be canvassed now. Speaking as a candidate, I can't be expected to accept the view that other names ought to be considered at this late stage. I hope that the Senior Tutor agrees with me."

from The Masters by C.P.Snow

14 Fill in the blanks in the following excerpt from a newspaper article choosing some of the reporting verbs from this list.

accuse believe hint say want announce expect reveal think

> A police superintendent .... to be at the centre of allegations over the falsification of Kent Police's crime detection figures, has retired on grounds of ill-health, the force .... yesterday. It is .... he may still face a disciplinary tribunal, with others. Last September the force .... that disciplinary action was being taken against 35 officers... .
>
> *from The Observer*

15 Read this extract. Underline any direct questions and circle indirect statements.

> On drugs we asked two questions: "Which of the following drugs have you tried?" and "Which drug do you think most dangerous in terms of the effect it has on society?" Overall, 65 per cent claimed to have tried cigarettes, 17 per cent cannabis, 6 per cent solvents and 89 per cent alcohol. Two per cent claimed to have tried heroin (the bravado factor, you might suppose, being cancelled out by the reticence factor; 7 per cent refused to answer this question). But, worryingly, 3 per cent of under-14's claimed to have sampled it; and a huge 85 per cent of under-14's reckoned to have tried alcohol, with only 8 per cent thinking it harmful. Only four in ten of the over-19's thought heroin most harmful. The government clearly has a lot of educating to do.
>
> *from New Society*

8 Combining messages

1 (Paras. 8.4 to 8.5) Say whether the linking word used in each of the following
sentences is a subordinating conjunction or a co-ordinating conjunction.

co-ordinating

  a We froze **and** stood rooted to the spot.   . . . .

  b We wouldn't have got so uptight, **if** he hadn't kept nagging us.   . . . .

  c We decided to go ahead **even though** she was against it.   . . . .

  d Are we going direct to the hotel **or** will we get the chance to see the town?   . . . .

  e He was clearing up **while** we were chatting.   . . . .

  f They were young **but** relatively experienced.   . . . .

Time clauses

2 (Paras. 8.8 to 8.22) Decide which of the responses on the right are possible.
There is more than one in each case.

  i   Someone told me your mother's an
      engineer and your father works part- time.
      Is that right?

      a She became an engineer before I was born.
      b Before I was born she became an engineer.
      c When we will leave school my father will go
         back to full-time work.
      d After we will leave school my father will work
         full-time.
      e My father will go back to work full-time as
         soon as we leave school.
      f My father will go back to work full-time as
         soon as we leave school.

  ii What did you all do?

      a While the lecturer gave his talk I jotted down
         some notes.
      b I jotted down some notes while the lecturer
         gave his talk.
      c I jotted down some notes whilst lecture
         proceeded.
      d All the students distracted each other when
         the lecturer spoke.
      e We would distract each other as the lecturer
         started his talk.
      f As he started his talk we would distract
         each other.

  iii Did he return?

      a Yes, in May, by which time we had the news.
      b Yes, in May, by which time we had had the
         news.
      c Yes, in May, at which point we had the news.
      d Yes, in May, whereupon we had the news.
      e Yes, in May, after which we had the news.
      f Yes, in May, after which we'd had the news.

3 (Paras. 8.8 to 8.21) Rewrite the following sentences, changing the meaning as
little as possible.

  a Throughout my stay in France I only saw three boys I knew.

      All the time . . . . *I was in France, I only saw three boys I knew.* . . . .

   b On every occasion he wrote to me I failed to answer.

      Whenever . . . .

   c I heard the door slam and rushed downstairs immediately.

      As soon as . . . .

   d I had only just walked through the door when the phone rang.

      Hardly . . . .

   e He became a teacher when he left university.

      Ever since . . . .

4 Complete these sentences, using the time expressions below. Use each expression only once.

   long before now that since the last time when whenever

   a I have lived in this house . . . . *since* . . . . I was born.

   b . . . . I try to study I get interrupted.

   c She met Ian . . . . she worked here.

   d I'm feeling better . . . . I've finished.

   e . . . . we went to the cinema was in January.

   f It was about 10 o'clock last night . . . . they got in.

Conditional clauses

5 (Paras. 8.25 to 8.42) Choose up to four suitable endings in the right hand column for each of the sentence openings in the left hand column.

i	If it hadn't rained	**a**	the garden would need watering.
ii	If it didn't rain	**b**	the plants die.
iii	If it doesn't rain	**c**	the plants would have died.
iv	Unless it had rained	**d**	the plants could die.
v	Unless it rained	**e**	the plants could have died.
vi	Unless it rains	**f**	the garden wouldn't be so green.
vii	Even if it had rained	**g**	the plants would be dead.
viii	Even if it rained	**h**	the plants may die.
ix	Even if it rains	**i**	the plants will die.

	i	ii	iii	iv	v	vi	vii	viii	ix
a									
c									
e									
f									

6 (Paras. 8.25 to 8.42) Read this poem and underline all the conditional clauses.

> The Rum Tum Tugger is a Curious Cat:
> If you offer him pheasant he would rather have grouse.
> If you put him in a house he would much prefer a flat,
> If you put him in a flat then he'd rather have a house.
> If you set him on a mouse then he only wants a rat,
> If you set him on a rat then he'd rather chase a mouse.
>
> Yes the Rum Tum Tugger is a Curious Cat -
>   And there isn't any call for me to shout it:
>   For he will do
>   As he do do
>   And there's no doing anything about it!

from Old Possum's Book of Practical Cats by T.S.Eliot

7 (Paras. 8.25 to 8.42) * Complete these sentences.

a I'd be delighted if . . . .

b Unless the weather's bad this weekend . . . .

c Provided that my teacher helps . . . .

d I'm going out as soon as . . . .

e If I were given the chance . . . .

Reason clauses

8 (Paras. 8.49 to 8.53) Complete the following letter.

> Hillside Cottage,
> Tumbledown Row,
> Old South Downe
>
> 28 February
>
> Dear Sir,
>   I am writing to you . . . . we have still not received a reply to a letter we wrote to you more than two weeks ago. I regret to say that I am still not satisfied with the work done by your company.
>   Your workmen came yesterday . . . . you sent them to rectify their mistakes. They did, in fact, attempt to repair the roof, and . . . . this has been done I should feel happier. However, they made no attempt to replumb the extension I am still extremely dissatisfied.
>   They say they have done the plumbing, and . . . . there are pipes under the floorboards, this is true, but these pipes do not work. My suspicion is that they have not been correctly joined, and we have buckets ready . . . . water starts dripping through the floor of the extension down into our living room! In addition we have switched the electricity off . . . . the faulty wiring causes a fire!
>   We are looking forward to hearing your comments on this.
>   Yours faithfully.
>   Mrs B. O'Brien

Result clauses

9 (Paras. 8.54 to 8.64)
Complete the
following memo.

BODGER & SON
ALL FALLE DOWNE

Tom – please pass this message on to Dick and Harry. Mrs O'Brien has written again – please put your work right immediately . . . . she stops writing to me. I've been to see the extension in question and I agree with what she's said. She's . . . . dissatisfied that I wouldn't be surprised if she took us to court – but I don't blame her – the work is . . . . bad . . . . we'll all be out of a job if you don't do better! It was . . . . a straightforward job . . . . I can't believe such a mistake has been made.

So please get things sorted out, ... I'll have to see Dick and Harry myself. Please get in touch with them immediately.

ABodger

Concessive clauses

10 (Paras. 8.65 to 8.72) Complete the following telephone conversation.

Mr Bodger: Hello - Mrs O'Brien? Bodger here. I trust that the men have completed the work to your satisfaction now.

Mrs O'Brien: Well - they've been working, ... *though* . . . . I wouldn't say it was right. . . . . you've made an effort to get the work done, it's hardly adequate. And to be honest, we feel we should get our money back, ... you feel you can offer to do the work yourself.

Mr Bodger: What's the problem now?

Mrs O'Brien: I think you'd better come and see for yourself. What really annoys me is that . . . . the fact they've come back again and again, it's still far from perfect. They work just like anyone else, ... they take breaks every five minutes. You may find that . . . . other customers <u>don't</u> mind, <u>we've</u> had enough.

Mr Bodger: I'll come over and inspect the work right now.

Clauses of place and manner

11 (Paras. 8.73 to 8.82) Complete the following dialogue.

Mrs O'Brien: Well, Mr Bodger I can't thank you enough for giving up all your time. It looks even better
............*than*....... we'd hoped. You've done the work exactly .... we wanted.

Mr Bodger: I'm sorry - I can only apologise for the trouble you've had. I can't work out why they behaved

.... they did. I feel .... I have no control over their work.

.... I've looked, they've made mistakes.

Mrs O'Brien: Some of this work, ... you yourself said, should have been quite

straightforward. Now it's .... I would expect in my own house. I'm not sure

whether they'll get any more work from me. They've behaved .... they

don't want a job, that's for certain.

Review : Adverbial clauses

12 (Para. 8.6) Describe the adverbial clauses in the following sentences.

i	She does exercise after exercise so as to perfect her English.	**a** TIME CLAUSE
ii	I turned up at the dentist's in spite of having the flu.	**b** CONDITIONAL CLAUSE
iii	He did the work very carefully so that he'd be sure of getting it right.	**c** PURPOSE CLAUSE
iv	We kept on working till the end of the day.	**d** REASON CLAUSE
v	She had a lot of loose change in case they ran out.	**e** RESULT CLAUSE
vi	There was too much noise where we were sitting.	**f** CONCESSIVE CLAUSE
vii	I wouldn't enrol for the course unless I felt it would fulfill my needs.	**g** PLACE CLAUSE
viii	In the interview, I tried to speak just as I do normally.	**h** CLAUSE OF MANNER

i	ii	iii	iv	v	vi	vii	viii
c							

13 (Paras. 8.6 to 8.82) Underline the adverbial clauses in the following extracts.

a And although cast adrift while he pursued other interests, other plans, she was waiting
for him, as one waits for an enemy; once they met, she would, by dint of insult and
outrage, reawaken the fury that had once been between them.

from Hotel du Lac by Anita Brookner

b They are dark caves. Even when they open towards the sun, very little light penetrates
down the entrance tunnel into the circular chamber. There is little to see, and no eye to
see it, until the visitor arrives for his five minutes, and strikes a match.

from A Passage to India by E.M.Forster

c Only when he reached Liverpool Street was he aware of hunger. He bought himself a
coffee and roll before catching the train home. It was nearly four before he put his key
in the latch. ..... Although it was still early, he felt very weary and his legs ached.

from Innocent Blood by P.D.James

71

Relative clauses

14 (Paras. 8.83 to 8.88) Say whether the relative clauses below are **defining** or **non-defining**.

a Rome, which is the capital of Italy, lies on the Tiber. ....*non-defining*........

b The city which he lives in is the largest in Central America. ....

c That actor, like many who are in the public eye, feels the pressure of the press. ....

d The boy who I spoke to was very co-operative. ....

e The island which is off the east coast of New York is called Long Island. ....

f The island, which lies in the Pacific Ocean, has a population of only 5,000. ....

g I don't want to speak to anyone who phones after 10.30pm. ....

Relative pronouns in defining clauses

15 (Paras. 8.89 to 8.91) Write sentences including **defining relative clauses**, using the information in brackets.

a The postman (he has dark hair) is always early.
   The postman who has dark hair is always early. ....

b The postman (I like him the best) always waves and smiles.
   ....

c The computer (it works best) costs £800.
   ....

d The computer (I've recommended it) is very efficient.
   ....

Relative pronouns in non-defining clauses

16 (Paras. 8.92 to 8.94) Write sentences including **non-defining relative clauses** using the information in brackets.

a The garden (it's south-facing) is almost 100 metres long.
   The garden, which is south-facing, is almost 100 metres long. ....

b The garden (we landscaped it ourselves) is very green at the moment.
   ....

c My mother (she visits me regularly) helps look after the children.
   ....

d My mother (the children love her) keeps them amused for hours.
   ....

17 (Paras. 8.83 to 8.108) Decide which of the following responses are possible.

i Who reported the accident?
- a The policeman who witnessed it.
- b A policeman, who witnessed it.
- c The policeman what was on the corner.
- d A policeman what was on the corner.
- e A policeman, who I gave all the details to.
- f The policeman I gave all the details to.

ii What did you think of the candidates?
- a The woman was the best candidate we interviewed.
- b The woman was the best candidate who we interviewed.
- c The woman was the best candidate that we interviewed.
- d Everyone we interviewed was well qualified.
- e Everyone we interviewed, was well qualified.
- f Everyone which we interviewed, was well qualified.

iii Who was that woman?
- a She's the one I lent my book to.
- b She's the one who I lent my book to.
- c She's the one whom I lent my book to.
- d She's the one to whom I lent my book.
- e She owns the shop which I go to.
- f She owns the shop to which I go to.

Iv Why are you going to work in a different hospital?
- a I'd prefer a hospital whose administration is better.
- b I'd prefer a hospital of which the administration is better.
- c I'd prefer a hospital whose environment is friendlier.
- d I'd prefer a hospital with whose staff I'd be happier.
- e I'd prefer a hospital whose staff I'd be happier with.
- f I'd prefer a hospital with whose staff I'd be happier with.

Additional points about non-defining relative clauses

18 (Paras. 8.109 to 8.111) Rewrite the following sentences so that they include relative clauses.

a I gave the letter to George. George then posted it for me.

I gave the letter to George, who posted it for me. ....

b You might find the exam too difficult. In this case, do what you can.

....

c A friend told her to improve her diet. At this point she made a huge effort to eat more healthily.

....

d She gave up cigarettes last year. By this time she had been smoking for 10 years.

....

e Some people can't swim. This means they may get nervous on a boat.

....

Non-finite clauses

19 (Paras. 8.132 to 8.133) Choose the ending in the right hand column which best completes each sentence opening in the left hand column.

i	Everyone going on the holiday	a	complained bitterly.
ii	The dog wearing a red collar	b	could be stopped.
iii	Any learner driver failing to display L-plates	c	is my father.
iv	No one wearing shorts	d	is trying to cross the road.
v	Someone wearing a stocking over his face	e	is doing a very good job.
vi	Any driver failing to stop at a zebra crossing	f	looked really excited.
vii	The boy preparing the barbeque	g	belongs to my mother.
viii	Everyone waiting in the queue	h	will be allowed into the mosque.
ix	Someone carrying a white stick	i	robbed the bank.
x	The man wearing the new suit	j	will be in big trouble.

i	ii	iii	iv	v	vi	vii	viii	ix	x
f									

Other structures used like non-finite clauses

20 (Paras. 8.134 to 8.136) Join each pair of sentences to make a simple sentence.

a John gave us the documents. They were neatly folded and filed.

John gave us the documents, neatly folded and filed. ....

b I was absolutely baffled. I reread the extract.

....

c The children sat down obediently. Their eyes were on the food.

....

d She was looking unkempt. Her skirt was crumpled and creased.

....

e I felt shocked by the news. I tried to work out what needed to be done.

....

Co-ordination

21 (Paras. 8.137 to 8.181) Use co-ordinating conjunctions to fill the gaps in the following sentences.

a She seemed calm .... *yet* ..... sad.

b Be good, ... you'll get into trouble.

c Everyone around him was panicking, ... he stayed calm.

d Ten people were killed . . . . twenty injured.

e We stayed in a comfortable . . . . shabby place.

f We didn't eat . . . . drink.

Emphasizing co-ordinating conjunctions

22 (Paras. 8.182 to 8.187) Join the pairs of sentences using emphasizing co-ordinating conjunctions.

    a I drive an estate car. My husband drives an estate car too.

       Both my husband and I drive estate cars.

    b Juliette wasn't there. John wasn't there.

    . . . .

    c I felt physically exhausted. I felt mentally exhausted.

    . . . .

    d You can put it in the oven. You can put it in the microwave.

    . . . .

    e I was disappointed. I was hurt.

    . . . .

    f She didn't feel delighted. She didn't feel upset.

    . . . .

9 Making texts

Referring back

1 (Paras. 9.2 to 9.5) Say which of the underlined pronouns and determiners refer back to something that has already been mentioned, and what they refer back to. If they do not refer back, leave the right hand column blank.

The cat joined the Re-education

Committee and was very active in **it** for some   it = *the Re-education Committee*
She = ...
days. **She** was seen **one** day sitting on a roof   one = ...

and talking to some sparrows who were just out   her = ...
She = ...
of **her** reach. **She** was telling **them** that **all**   them = ...
all = ...

animals were now comrades and that any sparrow

who chose could come and perch on **her** paw; but   her = ...
the = ...
the sparrows kept **their** distance.   their = ...

from Animal Farm by George Orwell

Referring back in a specific way

2 (Paras. 9.7 to 9.10) Insert 'this', 'that', 'these' or 'those' into the following dialogues.

a 'Happy Birthday! .... *This* .... is for you - open it now!'

'Oh! Thank you! .... are my favourite chocolates!'

b 'What's .... moving outside in the garden?'

'It's one of the squirrels that live in .... big tree over there. Haven't you ever seen one before?'

c 'The hotel's bad - the weather's awful! What a holiday! .... is the end!

'Well - I told you the weather was unpredictable here.

The only person you have to blame for .... is yourself!'

'................. 's what you always say!'

3 (Paras. 9.11 to 9.19) Use the following words and phrases to fill in the gaps.

above   the former   the latter   previous   then   thus   in this way

a I have just received my order of a washing machine and tumble dryer. While I am delighted with .... *the former* ......, I am disappointed with ....

76

b The . . . . chapter in this book covers the theme of combining messages.

c The exercise . . . . was easy - you should have got all the answers right.

d He wrote a cheque for too large an amount, ... incurring a debt of £1,500.

e Her English is much better than it was last year - but she didn't have a very good teacher

. . . .

f Dig a hole like this, and fill it with water. If you plant the bulbs . . . . , they should do well.

4 (Para. 9.20) Use the words in brackets to make new sentences.

a She gave an interesting impression of the film.

Her interpretation of the film was interesting. . . . . (**interpretation**)

. . . . (**view**)

b He judged the situation very well.

. . . . (**assessment**)

. . . . (**evaluation**)

c I've decided that this is no good.

. . . . (**conclusion**)

. . . . (**decision**)

Now write similar sentences, choosing other nouns from the list in paragraph 9.20.

. . . .

. . . .

. . . .

. . . .

. . . .

5 (Para. 9.21) Complete the sentence openings in the left hand column with endings from the right hand column.

i	In the circumstances	**a**	in the company?
ii	What is the latest development	**b**	of asking for help?
iii	Is there any possibility	**c**	as it is in theory?
iv	Is it as good in practice	**d**	on the situation?
v	It's a terrible state of affairs	**e**	of cause and effect.
vi	This is a feature	**f**	you'd better stay in bed.
vii	What is your position	**g**	of modern industrial society.
viii	This is a process	**h**	when old people are left alone.

i	ii	iii	iv	v	vi	vii	viii
f							

6 (Para. 9.23) Write down which pieces of writing from the list in paragraph 9.23 could be found in the following.

  a play ....*excerpt, extract, passage, quotation, text, words*..

  b magazine ....

  c page ....

  d list ....

  e maths book..

  f dictionary ....

  g exam paper..

Substituting for something already mentioned : using 'so' and 'not'

7 (Paras. 9.24 to 9.27) Fill in the longer gaps with reporting verbs from the list in paragraph 9.26. Insert 'so', 'not', or 'do so' into the shorter gaps.

  a Do you think it's going to rain? Yes, I ....*think*.......... ....*so*.... !

  b Are the exam results coming out soon? We certainly ....!

  c On the driving test he was .... to turn left, but he failed to ....

  d Should we go now? Yes, I ....

Comparing with something already mentioned

8 (Para. 9.38) Use your Cobuild dictionary if necessary to decide which of the words in bold would be most appropriate in the following sentences.

  a She wore a red suit with red shoes and a **corresponding/matching** hat. Her jacket, however, was in a **contrary/contrasting** colour.
  b He's moved and changed his job - the hours are much the same as in his old job and his salary is **analogous/comparable** too.
  c We've received two complaints about the meeting, but they are **analogous/unrelated** to each other.
  d In the discussion with the couple we found it hard to resolve their **conflicting/opposing** views. They're getting a divorce as they feel they are not **comparable/compatible**.
  e We see him every day as we work in **adjacent/parallel** offices.

Referring forward

9 (Paras. 9.41 to 9.48) Underline all the words in these sentences which refer forward to what is going to be said.

  a Students will not find <u>this</u> exercise difficult at all.

  b I told you to be prepared for such a situation as this.

  c My suitcase contained the following : clothes, wash bag, towel, presents.

  d This is what you need to do : read the text carefully, then answer the questions.

  e The following example includes a determiner.

  f At the top of the page were these words : 'Write clearly in ink'.

  g In the next exercise, you need to fill in the gaps.

10 (Paras. 9.41 to 9.48) Complete the following sentences with suitable words, to refer forward.

a I'd like you to do .... *the next* .... exercise, then have a break.

b The .... chapter is about the structure of information.

c The section .... is on ellipsis.

d Practise writing .... sentences as these.

e .... are the things you need: a pencil, a ruler, some paper.

Leaving out words : ellipsis

11 (Paras. 9.49 to 9.62) Complete the gaps below using the appropriate form of an auxiliary such as 'be', 'can', 'do' or 'have', adding 'not' where appropriate.

a He's a great deal taller than his sister .... *is* ....

b Most of them passed, but a few of them ....

c They had walked much further than we ....

d He had far more for breakfast than we ....

e I'd rather go now, but she ....

f You can run much faster than I ....

12 (Paras. 9.49 to 9.62) Decide which of the responses on the right are possible. There is more than one in each case.

i   I'm going to help out.
  a You needn't do.
  b You needn't.
  c Thanks, you need.
  d You'd better.
  e Don't unless you want to.
  f Don't unless you want.

ii You've got to do it.
  a I can't!
  b I couldn't!
  c I mustn't!
  d I haven't!
  e I don't!
  f I won't!

iii We could try to go there.
  a We daren't.
  b We daren't go there.
  c We need to.
  d We need.
  e We needn't go there.
  f We needn't.

iv I think it was him.
  a It can't have.
  b It can't have been.
  c It must have been.
  d It might have.
  e It must have.
  f It must have been.

Ellipsis in conversation

13 (Paras. 9.63 to 9.67) Find three possible responses for each of the questions or statements on the left.

i	She's got hepatitis.	**a** A lot!
ii	Is she very ill?	**b** I'm afraid so!
iii	How many are there?	**c** What?
iv	Are you pleased?	**d** Terribly!
		e 600!
		f Has she?
		g Not really!
		h Delighted!
		i Too many.

i	ii	iii	iv
c			
f			
g			

14 (Paras. 9.68 to 9.69) Suggest as many suitable responses as you can which agree with the following statements.

a I was absolutely fascinated.

So was I.
I was too.
Really?
What!

b I didn't have much to eat!

....
....
....
....

c I'd better go straight away.

....
....
....
....

d I'd never try that again.

....
....
....
....

10 The structure of information

Focusing on the thing affected : the passive voice

1 (Paras. 10.10 to 10.11) Explain why the agent is not mentioned in these sentences.

   a In the lab, the eggs **are mixed** with sperm. When they **have been fertilised**, they divide.   *processes and scientific experiments*

   b The distance **can be covered** in about two hours. ....

   c She **had been given** an injection and her tooth **had been filled**. ....

   d Metal **is heated** to a very high temperature and **is** then **poured** into the moulds. ....

   e English **is spoken** here. ....

2 (Paras. 10.9 to 10.15) Rewrite the following sentences in the passive.

   a She used a ladle to serve the soup.
       The soup was served with a ladle. ....

   b A number of teachers have debated this decision.

       ....

   c Frequent watering will develop good blooms.

       ....

   d Somebody's calling you.

       ....

   e They say that fibre is good for your health.

       ....

3 (Para. 10.16) Choose the opening in the left hand column which goes best with the phrase on the right, adding 'with', 'by', or 'in', as necessary.

i	The garden was overrun ... *with*	**a** his son.
ii	He's involved	**b** dozens of pieces of furniture.
iii	His beliefs are embodied	**c** crowds of people cheering.
iv	Albert Bridge is illuminated	**d** several shady deals.
v	Her happiness was overshadowed	**e** weeds.
vi	The streets were thronged	**f** her mother's illness.
vii	The room was crammed	**g** thousands of light bulbs.

i	ii	iii	iv	v	vi	vii
e						

4 (Para. 10.18) Referring to the lists in paragraph 10.18, fill in the gaps below, using the most appropriate tense of the passive.

   a In wartime, food . . . . *is* . . . . usually . . . . *rationed* . . . .

   b The doctor . . . . recently for unprofessional conduct.

   c She . . . . by the din.

   d The three demonstrators . . . . £50 each.

   e He . . . . widely . . . . for his paintings.

   f Unfortunately the football match . . . .

5 (Paras. 10.8 to 10.24) Underline all the passive forms in the following newspaper extract.

> More rain is forecast for the next few days.
>
> Last night all shipping in the English Channel and the Solent was advised to seek shelter and cross-channel ferries were hit. Many roads remained closed all over the country, and rail services, particularly in the west, will be disrupted for several days.
>
> Four trainee marines were treated for hypothermia after being airlifted by RAF helicopter from Dartmoor. The cost of damage from the floods this winter is now being counted in millions in the South-West and Wales.
>
> *from The Guardian*

Selecting focus : cleft sentences

6 (Paras. 10.25 to 10.30) Rewrite the following sentences.

   a She first heard the news from Francis.

     It. *was Francis who first told her the news.* . . . .

   b My brother is ill, not my sister.

     It. . . . .

   c Their generosity was what amazed me.

     What . . . .

   d They want more money.

     What . . . .

   e An open mind on the subject is the only thing you need.

     All. . . . .

Taking the focus off the subject : using impersonal 'it'

7 (Paras. 10.31 to 10.44) Say why the 'it' structure is used in each of the following sentences.

   a Will it be a problem if I stay? .... *whole situation implied* ....

   b It's really satisfying to learn something new. ....

   c It was a wet and windy March day. ....

   d I loathe it when people smoke. ....

   e It interests me that you don't find the work straightforward. ....

8 (Para. 10.36) * Use the adjectives in the second list in paragraph 10.36 to describe the weather in your country.

   a On a summer's day ....

   b In the spring ....

   c In the winter ....

   d At night ....

9 (Paras. 10.39 to 10.40) Choose the phrase in the right hand column which best completes each sentence opening in the left hand column.

i	It takes me		a	to learn new vocabulary as you meet it.
ii	It's important		b	an hour to get to school.
iii	It's a good idea		c	difficult to learn new words.
iv	It took a long time		d	to sort the problem out.
v	It costs		e	to take good care of your teeth.
vi	I find it		f	a lot to buy a season ticket.

i	ii	iii	iv	v	vi
b					

Introducing something new : 'there' as subject

10 (Paras. 10.46 to 10.55) Say why 'there' has been used in the following sentences.

   a There was a shrill scream outside. .... *something happened* ....

   b In the valley below there lay a small hut. ....

   c There is expected to be an agreement between the two sides shortly. ....

   d There are ten chapters in this book. ....

   e There was confusion among MPs about what the consequences might be. ....

   f There's no point even asking me - I won't do it. ....

Focusing on clauses or clause elements using adjuncts

11 (Para. 10.57) Decide which sentence adjunct in the left hand column goes best with each sentence in the right hand column. You can use the sentences more than once.

i	Miraculously,	**a**	that's exactly what I was thinking.
ii	Funnily enough,	**b**	the door opened but no-one was there.
iii	Mysteriously,	**c**	she was terribly generous.
iv	Characteristically,	**d**	everything turned out all right in end.
v	Typically,	**e**	the old lady survived the delicate operation.
vi	Fortunately,		
vii	Mercifully,		
viii	Curiously enough,		
ix	Luckily,		
x	Strangely enough,		

i	ii	iii	iv	v	vi	vii	viii	ix	x
d									

12 (Para. 10.61) Complete the sentences below with suitable sentence adjuncts from the list in paragraph 10.61.

a ..... *Rightly* .... or .... , I decided to go ahead.

b She .... offered to help us.

c They .... donated £500 to our collection.

d He .... gave the game away.

e She .... answered all the questions put to her.

13 (Para. 10.64) Using the list in paragraph 10.64, fill in the gaps in the following sentences.

a ..... *Officially* .... , the exchange rate is much lower than it is ....

b It is .... possible to cure a patient by using this form of treatment, but .... a cure has not yet been achieved.

c She's .... doing it for the sake of others but in my opinion she's .... only interested in herself.

d There is a worldwide campaign against the .... unacceptable use of pesticides.

e .... she is in charge of the project, but Jack does all the work.

f A long rest is .... the best remedy.

14 (Para. 10.68) Choose a word from the right hand column to complete each of the sentence openings in the left hand column.

i	The painting was aesthetically	a	superior.
ii	The new product is environmentally	b	strong.
iii	I'm sorry - I feel it's morally	c	viable.
iv	He believes that he is intellectually	d	composed.
v	Using detergents is ecologically	e	pleasing.
vi	It is financially	f	proven.
vii	He is wiry, but is physically	g	biased.
viii	I feel this plan is politically	h	unsound.
ix	He was angry, but was outwardly	i	safe.
x	It has been scientifically	j	wrong.

i	ii	iii	iv	v	vi	vii	viii	ix	x
e									

15 (Para. 10.70) Use the sentence adjuncts in brackets to rewrite the following sentences, keeping the meaning similar.

a I should imagine that there are about 70 students.

At a rough estimate, there are about 70 students. . . . . (**at a rough estimate**)

b They usually come to classes every day.

. . . . (**as a rule**)

c A large number of them enjoy doing grammar.

. . . . (**for the most part**)

d If we take everything into consideration, they're very willing.

. . . . (**all in all**)

Showing connections : linking adjuncts

16 (Para. 10.77) Choose a suitable sentence from the right hand column to link with a sentence in the left hand column.

i	Your son has become very short-sighted.	a	Hence he has lost weight.
ii	His hearing has deteriorated.	b	Thus he should soon feel fitter and stronger.
iii	We've told him to take more exercise.	c	As a result he could do with a deaf aid.
iv	He's been getting more exercise.	d	Consequently he requires new lenses.
v	He has reduced his fat intake.	e	Accordingly he's taken up jogging.

i	ii	iii	iv	v
d				

Emphasizing

17 (Para. 10.85) Rewrite the following sentences, choosing sentence adjuncts from the list in paragraph 10.85 to emphasize their content.

a He has overspent his budget.

He has actually overspent his budget.
....

b The hotel didn't have a restaurant.

....

c I loved the trip on the river.

....

d It is very kind of you.

....

e Don't look at me like that.

....

Indicating the most relevant thing : focusing adverbs

18 (Para 10.87) Complete each sentence opening on the left with a suitable ending from those on the right.

i	The following candidates have done particularly	**a**	from Spain and Italy.
ii	There are a large number of students, predominantly	**b**	with orders for books and magazines.
iii	They deal principally	**c**	Mr James.
iv	I'd like to thank everybody present, but especially	**d**	on French and German.
v	I'll be concentrating mainly	**e**	in the Highlands.
vi	The film was set in Scotland, chiefly	**f**	well.

i	ii	iii	iv	v	vi
f					

19 (Para. 10.88) Choose suitable adverbs from the list in paragraph 10.88 to fill in the gaps below.

a He was .... *purely* ...... interested in fast cars.

b It is .... a matter of what your priorities are.

c I .... want some information on ferries please.

d Students are chosen .... on merit.

Review : Focusing on clauses or clause elements using adjuncts

20 (Paras. 10.56 to 10.91) Put these sentence adjuncts in the appropriate boxes.

accordingly	furthermore	nevertheless	subsequently
at the same time	incidentally	on the contrary	thereby
by contrast	in conclusion	positively	thus
by the same token	likewise	secondly	to put it midly
by the way	meanwhile	similarly	to sum it up
even	moreover	simultaneously	you know

INDICATING AN ADDITION	INDICATING A PARALLEL	CONTRASTS AND ALTERNATIVES
CAUSES *accordingly*	INDICATING A SEQUENCE IN TIME	ORDERING POINTS
INDICATING A CHANGE IN A CONVERSATION	EMPHASIZING	

Doing by saying : performative verbs

21 (Paras. 10.102 to 10.103) Using the lists in paragraphs 10.102 and 10.103, decide which performative verb would be most appropriate in each of the following statements.

a I . . . . *guarantee* . . . . . . the watch will work.

b I . . . . you to ten years' imprisonment.

c I . . . . that I ever said that.

d I . . . . Stephen as chairperson.

e I . . . . you for what you have done.

Making a statement into a question : question tags

22 (Paras. 10.110 to 10.114) Add suitable question tags to the following statements.

a He's been there before, ... *hasn't he* . . . . ?

b It arrived, ... ?

c Don't tell her, ... ?

d I'm doing quite well, ... ?

e See that it's finished, ... ?

f Let's go, ... ?

g You will let me know your results, ... ?

h It doesn't make sense, ... ?

Reference Section

Forming plurals of count nouns

1 (Paras. R2 to R8) Make the following nouns plural, and write them in the appropriate columns according to their pronunciation.

bag bank house cloth breed flash fox batch kit loss girder spear drain branch pit

/s/	/z/	/ɪz/
banks	bags	batches
....	....	....
....	....	....
....	....	....
....	....	....
....	....	....

2 (Paras. R2 to R19) Form plurals for the following count nouns.

a	loaf	*loaves*	**k**	disc	....
b	spark	....	**l**	ox	....
c	analysis	....	**m**	flamingo	....
d	pitch	....	**n**	crumb	....
e	mouse	....	**o**	class	....
f	badge	....	**p**	echo	....
g	nucleus	....	**q**	index	....
h	flea	....	**r**	fly	....
i	fireman	....	**s**	radius	....
j	stratum	....	**t**	vertebra	....

The spelling and pronunciation of possessives

3 (Paras. R32 to R40) Make possessive forms from the following.

a my parents dog ...*my parents' dog*...

b my mother and father house ....

c St Mary   school. . . . .

d the children   bags . . . .

e three people   passports. . . . .

f women   rights. . . . .

g Julie   camera. . . . .

4 (Para. R38) Add an apostrophe s ('s) to each of the following names, writing them in the appropriate columns according to their pronunciation.

Beth Liz Luke Madge Ralph Rod Ross Sue William

/s/	/z/	/ɪz/
Beth's		

Numbers

5 (Para. R45) Punctuate these numbers.

a 63127

b 7384

c 3429860

d 179324

e 815699253

f 1634592

6 (Paras. R46 to R47) Write the ordinal number in full and give its abbreviation in brackets for each of the following cardinal numbers.

a 21   *twenty first (21st)* . . . .

b 45   . . . .

c 3   . . . .

d 122   . . . .

e 99   . . . .

f 58   . . . .

g 20   . . . .

h 300   . . . .

7 (Paras. R48 to R49) Write out the following fractions in full and then convert them to percentages.

a $^1/_2$ ...... *a half 50%* ....

b $^1/_4$ ....

c $^3/_4$ ....

d $^4/_{100}$ ....

e $^7/_{10}$ ....

Verb forms and the formation of verb groups

8 (Paras. R55 to R57) Make the 's' form of each of the following verbs, writing them in the appropriate columns according to their pronunciation.

arrive bath buzz drag finish fix forego infer judge leap loot pick puff reduce speed

/s/	/z/	/ɪz/
baths		

9 (Paras. R59 to R70) Write down the '–ing' and '-ed' forms of the following verbs.

a skip ...... *skipping* .... *skipped* ......

b stow ....

c spot ....

d man ....

e chew ....

f distil ....

g disagree ....

h confer ....

10 (Paras. R59 to R85) Make the '-ed' form of the following verbs, writing them in the appropriate column according to their pronunciation.

allude amass cry enliven enrich invent lap mash niggle peak raid ratify sprint spurt tickle

/t/	/ɪd/	/d/
amassed		

11 (Paras. R72; R78; R79) Write down as many verbs as you can whose past form and past participle are the same as their base form, both in spelling and pronunciation.

...*bet*..

....

....

....

....

....

....

....

12 (Para. R72) Write down the infinitive form of the verbs whose past form is written below.

a	...*shoot*... shot	**g**	.... stood
b	.... hid	**h**	.... strode
c	.... bound	**i**	.... told
d	.... thrust	**j**	.... did
e	.... rode	**k**	.... understood
f	.... trod	**l**	.... forbade

13 (Para. R79) Use a verb from the list in paragraph R79 in an appropriate tense to complete each of the following sentences.

a The meeting ......*has overrun*....... by 10 minutes.

b The insurers say that they .... the cargo.

c He .... a serious operation last month.

d You .... what I said - I said 'beard' - not 'beer'!

e The boy .... his shoes and needs new ones.

f I'm sorry I'm so late – I ....

g You .... my name. It should be S - T - E - A - R - N.

h The motor .... and the machine stopped working.

14 (Paras. R80 to R88) Decide what the contractions stand for in each of the following sentences.

a She's been on holiday five times this year!   's =   ...*has*...

b She's being terribly difficult at the moment.   's = ...

c She'd been to Australia before, you know.   'd = ...

d If we'd had the money, we'd have bought it at the time.   'd = ...

                                                             'd = ...

Finite verb groups and the formation of tenses

15 (Paras. R89 to R119) Say which tense is used in each of the following active sentences.

a I live in London. .... *simple present*

b He was painting the room last night. ....

c They'd never heard of it. ....

d We're watching TV at the moment. ....

e I've been to Italy three times. ....

f He came round for a chat yesterday. ....

g We'll be lying on a beach this time next week. ....

16 (Paras. R89 to R119) Say which tenses are used in these passive sentences.

a Cheese is made in Switzerland. .... *simple present*

b The proposal was being discussed yesterday. ....

c Things will have been sorted out by then. ....

d He had been stabbed. ....

e Their problems have been greatly exaggerated. ....

Forming adverbs

17 (Paras. R136 to R146) Write down the adverbs related to the following adjectives and nouns.

a shy   *shyly* ....   **h** satisfactory ....

b fortnight   ....   **i** outright   ....

c easy   ....   **j** deep   ....

d gentle   ....   **k** eerie   ....

e straight   ....   **l** freelance   ....

f tragic   ....   **m** crooked   ....

g purpose   ....   **n** wry   ....

Key

Note: Exercises marked with a star (*) do not have answers in the key.

Chapter 1

1
- a modifier
- b common noun
- c conjunction
- d specific determiner
- e proper noun
- f personal pronoun
- g indefinite pronoun
- h quantifier
- i demonstrative pronoun
- j general determiner

2
- a journeys
- b calves
- c men
- d mouths
- e shellfish
- f mice
- g babies
- h zebra
- i thoughts
- j gallows

3
- a watch
- b toad
- c woman
- d country
- e dice
- f raft
- g hovercraft
- h bus
- i grapefruit
- j species

4
- i b, is
- ii g, causes
- iii h, travels
- iv i, involves/is
- v f, cooks
- vi a, has
- vii c, is
- viii d, grows
- ix e, involves

5 Possible sentences :

| i c,d | ii b,c | iii b,d | iv b,c | v b,d | vi b,c |
| vii b,c | viii a,d | ix b,c | x b,d |

6 Example answer :

The local press is very concerned about the present situation in schools. The government is cutting back on education, although the opposition is strongly opposed to the cuts. The local council claims that schools are not affected. However, local schools are deteriorating. In the schools staff are suffering a drop in morale, and the community is up in arms about the situation. The public are very dissatisfied, as they consider that the family unit is affected.

7
- a is
- b are, are
- c have
- d has
- e is, its
- f are
- g consists
- h are, their

8

Family	Honorary titles	Royalty	Church
Miss	Dame	Prince	Archbishop
Mr	Baron	Princess	Bishop
Mrs	Baroness	King	Brother
Ms	Lady	Queen	Cardinal
	Lord		Father
			Pope

Hospital	Police	Military
Doctor	Constable	Admiral
Mr	Inspector	Colonel
Nurse	Police Constable	Corporal
Professor	Sergeant	General
Sister		Lieutenant
		Major
		Private
		Sergeant

9 Possible answers :
- a false / first / general / personal
- b different / modern
- c new / recent
- d latest / next / previous / second
- e incredible
- f previous
- g different
- h certain

10 P beginning, feeling
T meeting, warning, sightseeing, sitting/studying, window-shopping

11
- a inverted commas
- b bank account, telephone number
- c burglar alarm, police station
- d blood pressure, X-ray
- e package holiday, traveller's cheques, car park, air conditioning
- f high school, modern languages, book token
- g post office, letter box
- h greenhouse effect
- i brain drain
- j compact disc, hire purchase, value added tax

12 bed, mother, case, prison, suit, London, gloves, underclothes, shoulder bag, toilet articles, pyjamas, extravagance, necessities, living, Phillipa, Phillipa, case, mother, middle, stream, way, tow-path, splash, case, water, body, road

13
- a hair, is
- b advice, was/has been
- c trousers, have split
- d news, is/was
- e suburbs, are
- f flock, numbers/numbered
- g knowledge, is increasing, progress, is/has been
- h music, helps

14

it	=	the plane
their	=	the children's
you	=	husband
them	=	the presents
them	=	the children
I	=	Sue
my	=	Sue's
their	=	the friend's
I	=	Helen
them	=	the friend
their	=	no-one's
you	=	Steve
them	=	the postcards
theirs	=	everyone's postcards
ours	=	John and Mary's postcards
they	=	John and Mary's friends
our	=	John and Mary's
we	=	John and Mary

15 a himself, he
b itself
c himself/herself, his/her/their
d I, myself, my, me
e ourselves, our

16 nothing, anything, something, everyone/everybody,
everyone/everybody, no-one/nobody, everyone/everybody/
everything

no-one/nobody/nothing, no-one/nobody, someone/
everyone/everybody, anyone/anything, No-one/Nobody,
Everyone/Everybody, someone/something, everyone's/
everybody's

17 a   one   =   a cup
         one   =   a cup
   b   one   =   a cake
        the others   =   two cakes
   c   one   =   people in general/ we
   d   one's   =   this cup
   e   one   =   a man
        another   =   a different man
   f   one   =   a person
        one   =   the other person
   g   each   =   one person and the other(s)
   h   one   =   a recipe
        the other   =   a different recipe
   i   each   =   individually

18 They, they, they, their, them, they, their

herself, her, she, He, his, the, they, his

19 many/some, some/other/many, the, every, the, the, the, the,
the, Every, No, Many, few, many/most

20 a the Far East   b either
   c the violin   d the stage, the theatre
   e the church   f church
   g either, the economy

21 a a, -, the
   b the, a, the/-, -
   c the, an, the, a
   d the, a, the/a, the/-, -, -, the

22 a She paid them twice the sum they asked for.
   b They paid me half the sum I'd asked for.
   c Both Sebastian and William were enjoying themselves.
   d He's now earning double/twice the salary he was earning.
   e All the family opened their Christmas presents.

23 a The, the/this, all, all, -, -, -, -, The/One, -, the, the, -, -,
     the, -, -, -
   b One, his, a, the, the/a, the, a, -, the, a, the, The/A, a, the,
     an, the, his/the, -, a, the, the, the

24 One, her, She, the, she, she, she, her, they, her, they, the

Chapter 2

1 sweet, seaside, wet, red, shrimping, slippery, seaweedy,
small, clear, grey, translucent, beautiful, green

2 a velvet : attributive
   b shattered : predicative
   c old : attributive
   d hard : attributive
   e sparkling white : attributive

3 a busy
   b attractive, pleasant, patient, understanding, different
   c fine, warm, pleasant
   d difficult, hard, simple, easy, silly
   e anxious, worried, appropriate

4 Adjectives not possible:
official, north, military, south, commercial, theoretical,
domestic, natural, personal, regular

5 i f   ii a   iii e   iv c   v h   vi g
vii d   viii b

6 Appropriate adjectives :
i a,b,c,d   ii b,c,d   iii b,d,e,f

7 Marie's card :
perfect, utter/absolute/total, complete/real, entire
Katy's card :
perfect, absolute/utter, complete, outright

8 a the other
   b the two remaining
   c our own particular / specific
   d your present / main
   e her entire
   f my last / only (remaining)

9 a remedial teacher
   b forensic medicine
   c neighbouring village
   d fleeting glance
   e belated congratulations
   f cardiac failure
   g thankless task
   h preconceived ideas

11 a inclined to
   b willing/unwilling/bound to
   c confident/sure/certain, worried/afraid/anxious that
   d bound/sure/certain to
   e willing/happy to
   f bound/sure/certain to

12 a most delicious roast
   b modern grey concrete
   c pretty red and white chequered
   d ordinary light brown straight

13 charming, interesting, tiring, boring, encouraging,
intimidating, depressing, overwhelming, astounding,
refreshing, welcoming

14 i b   ii g   iii h   iv j   v c   vi a
vii f   viii d   ix e   x i

15 a She was intrigued by the situation.
   b The show is destined to be a flop.
   c He is preoccupied by his own problems.
   d He wasn't disposed to help us.
   e I am indebted to my parents.

16 a bullet-proof
    b labour-saving, interest-free
    c purpose-built, red-brick
    d audio-visual
    e long-distance
    f second-hand, lead-free
    g mass-produced
    h two-faced

17 Comparative : a,b,d,f,g
    Superlative : c,e,h

18 a Country lanes are narrower than motorways.
    b My brother is a lot older than me.
    c Sam is much shorter than Billy.
    d The swimming pool is shallower than the village pond.
    e Mike's suitcase is heavier than Joe's.

19 GREATEST SNOWFALL, HEAVIEST HAILSTONES, WETTEST
    PLACE, DRIEST PLACE, the longest, HIGHEST SHADE
    TEMPERATURE, HOTTEST PLACE, COLDEST PLACE, The
    lowest, FASTEST SURFACE WIND SPEED, WINDIEST PLACE

20 a trouser pocket
    b arms race
    c scissor blades
    d binoculars case
    e jeans belt
    f troop movement

21 a I've, brother's, St Mary's, sisters'
    b Miss Williams', Mrs James's
    c brother-in-law's, friends'/friend's
    d sheep's
    e shops', supermarkets'

22 a a great deal of
    b A number of, lots of
    c heaps of/tons of/lots of
    d a good deal of/a great deal of/tons of/heaps of/lots of
    e Many of/The majority of, some of/a number of
    f a number of
    g lots of/heaps of
    h the whole of/the majority of, lots of/heaps of

23 a salt   b glass
    c butter   d grass
    e rubbish   f honey
    g beer   h flour
    i whisky   j dirt
    k evidence   l lemon

24 a basket/bowl/tin   b tank
    c bottle/carton   d tube
    e bottle   f barrel/bottle/can/crate
    g sack/bag   h packet/tub
    i bar   j jar

25 a A chair is a piece of furniture.
    b A suitcase is an item of luggage.
    c A dress is an article of clothing.
    d A news story is a piece of information.

26 a He's in his thirties.
    b He's in his late seventies.
    c She's in her early forties.
    d They're in their teens.

27 a There are roughly 800 students in my school.
    b Approximately half of them live in (the) town and half in the
      country.
    c Something like 20% of them live on farms and nearly all
      their fathers grow crops.
    d The surrounding farms are 800 years old or thereabouts.

    e There are more than 200 farms around the town.
    f The local population is roughly 3,000.

29 a collision with   b contribution to
    c aptitude for   d dissatisfaction with
    e embargo on/ ban on   f provision for
    g grudge against   h sympathy with
    i curb on   j debate on

30 a opportunity/chance
    b desire/readiness/willingness
    c ability
    d chance/opportunity
    e need

31 Adjectives :
    circular, uncertain, interesting, dull, difficult, human,
    surrounding, passing, extraordinary

    Expressions referring to measurements or quantities :
    eight feet long, five feet high, three feet wide, twenty feet,
    two, three, four, fourteen, twenty-four, Nothing, nothing, one

Chapter 3

1 **a** economized **b** was yawning, is dozing
   c arise **d** shivered
   e crackled **f** has elapsed

2 **a** welcomed
   b shocked, reported
   c built / is building / has built / had built
   d Address, take
   e pronounced
   f displays / displayed / has displayed

3 Intransitive : a, f
   Transitive : b, c, d, e, g

4 Intransitive : **a** i **b** ii **c** ii **d** i **e** i
   Transitive : **a** ii **b** i **c** i **d** ii **e** ii

5 inserted(T), found(T), smelled, overlaid(T), was, told(T),
   led, gave(T)

6 **i** c, f **ii** d, e **iii** a, b **iv** c, f

7 **a** approached
   b reached / entered / inhabited
   c occupy
   d reached, approached / neared
   e filled / thronged

8 **a** enjoy myself
   b dress himself
   c acclimatize ourselves
   d express herself

9 **i** made, c **ii** have, f
   iii making, g **iv** taken / made, e
   v held, h **vi** made, j
   iiv taking / taken, i **viii** gave, b
   ix take, d **x** made / gave, a

10 **a** i is hanging ii hanged **b** i, ii cheated
   c i, ii won **d** i, ii studied
   e i, ii had driven **f** i are striking ii struck

11 the door, the knocking, it, it, possiblities, a song, a song, the
   song, us

12 **i** j **ii** i **iii** g **iv** f **v** b
   vi c **vii** d **viii** e **ix** a **x** h

13 **a** has sold well.
   b quickened as the light began to fail.
   c melted in a saucepan.
   d rocked gently.

14 **a** had corresponded with
   b to communicate with
   c hugged / cuddled / embraced, kissed
   d argued with / fought with

15 **a** to, to, -, -, - **b** for, to, to, - **c** -, to

16 True :
   i a, c, e, f, g
   ii b, c, d, e, f
   iii b, c, d, e, g

17 Inappropriate :
   a pack off **b** weed out
   c doll up **d** frighten away
   e hammer out **f** smooth over
   g shoot down **h** add up

18 **a** took off **b** threw up
   c set out **d** looked up

19 **a** woke up. **b** wakes up at 8am.
   c has closed down. **d** will check in at 1.30.

20 **a** answers her back. **b** tell them apart.
   c talked her round. **d** invited them in.

21 **i** c her **ii** b them **iii** a it **iv** f it
   v h it **vi** e him **vii** d him **viii** g them

22 **a** ii **b** i **c** iv **d** iii
   e vii **f** v **g** viii **h** vi

23 **a** had grown into **b** amounted to
   c turning into **d** turned to

24 **a** certified
   b was christened
   c was designated / was declared
   d is nicknamed
   e declared

25 **i** b **ii** a **iii** f **iv** e **v** c **vi** d

26 Correct : **a** i **b** i **c** ii **d** ii **e** i **f** ii

27 **a** listening to, reading
   b watched, playing
   c expect, to do
   d persuaded, to take
   e kept, waiting
   f heard, singing
   g encouraged, to develop
   h expected, to obey

Chapter 4

1 give information : a, g
obtain information : b, h
express an opinion : c, l
give an order : f, j
make a promise : e, k
make a suggestion : d, i

2 a I'd like (Declarative)
b Write down (Imperative)
c Have you taken (Interrogative)
d Speak up (Imperative)
e He jotted down (Declarative)
f Do it (Imperative)
g He'll pop round (Declarative)
h did you think? (Interrogative)

3 i f, b   ii k, t   iii a, j   iv l, i   v h, r
vi m, p   vii d, o   viii e, n   ix g, s   x c, q

4 i Are they American?
ii Have they lived/been living in London for a long time?
iii Have they got/Do they have many children?
iv Is their eldest child a boy or a girl?
v Do they often go to the States?
vi Are they planning/Do they plan to go to New York this year?

i e   ii a   iii c   iv f   v b   vi d

5 a i   Who invited you to the cinema last night?   S
    ii   Who was invited to the cinema last night?   O
  b i   Whose car is in the car park?   S
    ii   Where's your car?   O
  c i   Who read the book?   S
    ii   What did she read?   O
  d i   Who's writing another novel?   S
    ii   What's he writing?   O

6 a Compare   b Suppose
c Consider   d Imagine
e Picture   f Contrast
g Take

7 'It's a beautiful thing, the destruction of words. Of course the great wastage is in the verbs and adjectives, but there are hundreds of nouns that can be got rid of as well. It isn't only the synonyms; there are also the antonyms. After all, what justification is there for a word which is simply the opposite of some other word? A word contains its opposite in itself. Take "good", for instance. If you have a word like "good", what need is there for a word like "bad"? "Ungood" will do just as well - better, because it's an exact opposite, which the other is not. Or again, if you want a stronger version of "good", what sense is there in having a whole string of vague useless words like "excellent" and "splendid" and all the rest of them? "Plusgood" covers the meaning; or "doubleplusgood" if you want something stronger still. Of course we use those forms already, but in the final version of Newspeak there'll be nothing else. In the end the whole notion of goodness and badness will be covered by only six words - in reality only one word. Don't you see the beauty of that, Winston?' It was B.B.'s idea originally, of course' he added as an afterthought.

8 a Neither, nor   b never, nowhere/nothing
c No one/Nobody   d Neither/None   e no

9 a I don't want to eat late.
b I don't expect him to come.
c We aren't planning to go on holiday this year.
d I don't seem to have your full address.

10 a None of   b never   c nowhere
d not altogether/not very
e Never   f nothing but   g Neither

11 a inability/disability   b malpractice
c inaction   d misinformation
e irresponsibility   f non-co-operation
g anti-matter   h inefficiency
i illegibility   j irreverence
k inaccuracy   l counter-espionage
m ex-wife   n unhappiness
o mismanagement   p insincerity
q antihero   r impossibility
s ex-Prime Minister   t anti-apartheid

12 a immobile   b unaware
c inexplicably   d irreverent
e maladjusted   f counter-revolutionary
g anticlockwise   h immoral
i non-existent   j unproductive
k discourteously   l unreliable
m impractical   n illegal
o irrational   p disagreeable
q non-profit-making   r irreplaceable
s unnatural   t unremarkable

13 a undo   b defuse
c disconnect   d misinform
e untie   f disapprove
g mislay   h miscalculate
i unstick   j mistreat/maltreat
k decode   l counter-attack
m mislead   n declassify
o desensitize   p disobey
q misconstrue   r de-escalate
s misread   t disagree

14 i e   ii h   iii a   iv g
v f   vi b   vii d   viii c

15 a carless   b stateless
c penniless   d leafless
e jobless   f cloudless

16 hardly, seldom, rarely, scarcely, barely

17 a a bit / the least bit / at all
b a bit / at all / in the slightest
c nothing whatsoever
d whatsoever / at all
e at all / a bit / the least bit
f whatsoever / at all

19 a ought to (modal), daren't (semi-modal)
b might (modal), used to (semi-modal)
c needs (semi-modal), should (modal)
d shall (modal), can (modal)

20 a Will he arrive? / He won't arrive.
b Should we leave? / We shouldn't leave.
c Ought you to have written? / You oughtn't to have written.
d Would they have told me? / They wouldn't have told me.

21 i b, e   ii a, d
iii f, h   iv c, g

22 a 'll - present b wouldn't - past
c could - past d shall - future
e would - past

23 a awareness b capability (past)
c ability d awareness (past)
e ability (past) f capability

24 a could / may / might
b should / will / may
c must / should / will / ought to
d could / may / might
e could / may / might
f shall / will
g could / may / might

25 a can - permission
b may - formal permission
c can - permission
d could - permission in the past
e may - formal permission
f could - permission in the past

26 a mustn't / shouldn't / cannot
b shouldn't
c mustn't / shouldn't / cannot
d may not / shall not / mustn't / cannot
e will not

27 *See below*

28 Suggested answers:

a Can I make a phone call?
Could I make a phone call?
May I make a phone call?
Might I possibly make a phone call?

b Could you lend me £5.00?
Would you lend me £5.00?
Will you lend me £5.00?
Can you lend me £5.00?

c Please could you stop smoking?
Can you stop smoking?
Please would you stop smoking?
Will you please stop smoking?

d Would you like a cup of tea?
Have a cup of tea.
May I offer you a cup of tea?
Might I offer you a cup of tea?

e We could go outside.
Couldn't we go outside?
Shall we go outside?
Should we go outside?

f I won't talk about the accident.
I cannot talk about the accident.
I am not able to talk about the accident.
I will not talk about the accident.

g I'd like to go on holiday.
I'd love to go on holiday.
I should like to go on holiday.

h I should do it now.
I must do it now.
I shall have to do it now.

29 i a, b, c, f ii a, b, c, d iii a, c, d, f

30 i used to ii used to iii didn't used to
iv used to v didn't used to vi used to
vii used to viii didn't used to

i f ii d iii h
iv g v c vi a
vii e viii b

	can cannot	could could not	may may not	might might not	ought to ought not to
INDICATING ABILITY	X	X			
INDICATING LIKELIHOOD	X	X	X	X	X
INDICATING PERMISSION	X	X	X		
INDICATING UNACCEPTABILITY	X		X		

	shall shall not	should should not	will will not	would would not	must must not
INDICATING ABILITY					
INDICATING LIKELIHOOD	X	X	X	X	X
INDICATING PERMISSION					
INDICATING UNACCEPTABILITY	X	X	X		X

Chapter 5

1 i c : performative verbs used in commenting (5.16)
ii g : general truths (5.10)
iii f : general present including the present moment (5.9)
iv b : used in commentaries (5.14)
v e : used in reporting (5.15)
vi a : regular or habitual actions (5.11)
vii d : used in reviews (5.12)

2 **a** perform, earn **b** plays **c** ebbs, flows
d confess **e** enclose

3 i d : the moment of speaking (5.17)
ii e : emphasizing the present moment (5.18)
iii a : habitual actions (5.20)
iv c : frequent actions (5.24)
v b : progressive change (5.19)

5 are enjoying, do, walk/go, have/take, lie, are doing, is trying,
is pouring/is sprinkling, am writing are, look/am, are
learning, is, wish

6 The Little Calf is now eight months old. A human child at this
age is trying to lift its body from the floor, to cling briefly to
chairs, and to reach for the hem of mother's skirt. The Little
Calf, by contrast, is well along the road to independence, if
his mother were to disappear overnight he might perhaps
survive alone.

The Little Calf and his mother are feeding 400 miles at
sea off San Francisco. They will go no farther north this year,
though many of their companions have dropped from sight
over the horizon, far on their way to the Bering Sea. The
females that came into heat have dallied behind. The pattern
of the herd as the Little Calf knew it in spring is dissolving.
Whales of like age and sex and breeding disposition are
now consorting; the groups are separating in space
because of the differences in their swimming speeds.

The day is mild. A filmy diffusion pales the blue of the sky and
gives a soft extra light. A gentle breeze touches the moving
sea. Here and there the surface breaks in a pattern of light,
struck by a shower of needles. Schools of sauries, each
holding a million fish, break and boil to the top. Their sides
are gleaming iridescent silver; their backs are metallic blue-
green. The Little Calf and his mother, along with seven other
females, the harem bull, and a young male, are lazily
following the fish, feasting as they go. During the bright of
day, when the schools descend for reasons of their own -
reasons unknown to man - the old whales pursue them down,
during the night the young whales plunge with open jaws
through the silver masses. Even the Little Calf, though
nursing, is swallowing the fat, tasty, ten-inch fish.

7 **a** died, said, drank, died
b averted, put out
c tried, left, said, fell
d voted, reported
e used, was, attacked, clung, drove off
f did, affected

8 fell, fractured, was presenting, lost, slipped, went, was
feeling

9 **a** have undermined, have used
b has vowed, told, was
c jackknifed, spilled, have had

10 i b ii c iii a

11 **a** ever since
b ago
c yesterday evening, this morning
d all day

12 **a** past continuous - repeated actions (5.31)
b past perfect - event before a particular time in the
past (5.37)
c present perfect - no specific time stated (5.33)
d past simple - regular action (5.30)
e present perfect - situation still exists (5.35)
f past perfect - expectations and wishes (5.39)

14 **a** modal 'will' (5.53)
b 'be going to' (5.58)
c future continuous (5.55)
d 'will' - general truths (5.54)
e 'be due to' (5.59)
f future perfect continuous (5.57)
g simple present (5.65)
h present continuous (5.65)

15 i b ii d iii e iv c v a

16 **a** at once / immediately / instantly / within minutes / within
the hour
b eventually / finally / soon
c Eventually / Finally
d at once / immediately / later on / presently / within
minutes / within the hour

18 i a,c,d,e ii a,c,e,f iii a,c,e,f

19 **a** in, at, in **b** During, at
c in, during/over, At, on **d** by
e During, during/in

20 **a** seconds
b decades, century
c century
d months, year
e day, night
f minutes, hour

21 **a** intermittently / occasionally / sporadically / constantly /
frequently
b rarely / seldom, always / usually
c hardly ever / never
d from time to time / periodically
e ever, often / sometimes / occasionally

22 i c ii e iii b iv d v a

23 in, after, for/over, after, until, since, for, for

Chapter 6

1 a He's somewhat absent-minded.
b She's well known for her generosity.
c These scissors are simply useless.
d The house is normally kept meticulously clean.
e He really speaks loudly to the children. / He speaks to the children really loudly.
f They quickly remembered what they had been told.
g The children are usually very helpful in their own way.
h He frequently forgets to do his homework on time.

2 a hardly / scarcely
b hardly / scarcely
c presently / shortly
d lately
e presently / shortly

3
	i		ii	
a	i	clear	ii	clearly
b	i	direct	ii	directly
c	i	first	ii	first
d	i	easily	ii	easy
e	i	deep	ii	deeply

4 i b,d,e,f   ii a,b,c,d

5
i d	ii b	iii e	iv a
v h	vi g	vii f	viii c

6 a sincerely
b part-time, full-time
c instinctively
d bodily
e illegally, officially
f logically
g first-class / solo

7 a I've enjoyed all the lessons tremendously.
b I've really enjoyed all the lessons.
c He's lost virtually all his money.
d You knew perfectly well what I was talking about.
e I'm positively disgusted by her behaviour.
f He works reasonably hard - but he dreams a great deal.

9 Adverbs of manner :
angrily, beautifully, carefully, fiercely, meticulously, silently, vaguely

Adverbs of degree :
almost, badly, immensely, profoundly, somewhat, terribly, utterly, virtually, well, wonderfully

Adverbs of place:
abroad, ashore, downstairs, downstream, near, overseas, underfoot, underneath

10 a alongside, out of
b at, on
c beyond, next to
d Among

11 a hang on the hooks.
b belong in the drawer.
c stayed in (the house) after his illness.
d live in London.

13 *See plan – right*

14
i e	ii a	iii b	iv c
v f	vi d	vii g	

15 Suggestions :
The house was situated half a mile beyond the trees.
The children were lingering 20 metres behind our party.
The tent was pitched a couple of miles outside the town.
They were snorkelling a few metres from the shore.
The plane was circling a few thousand feet above the town.

16 a into   b toward / towards
c into / onto   d alongside
e around / round

17 i a,b,d,e   ii a,b,c,f   iii a,b,c,f

18 a downstairs   b outdoors
c near   d ashore
e upstairs   f indoors
g underground

19
i	b	round and round
ii	d	to and fro / up and down
iii	e	downhill
iv	c	across/over
v	f	upstream
vi	a	through

20 a i, v   b iv   c ii, vi   d iii

22 Prepositions:

FROM
to, from, with, in, to/from
TO

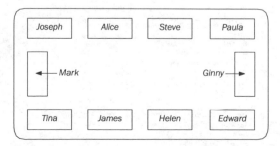

Chapter 7

1 a asked/inquired
  b ordered/yelled
  c exclaimed/whispered
  d boasted/declared
  e asked/inquired

2 agreed/promised, expected/thought, expected/thought, imagined/expected, found/learned/realised/saw, felt, reasoned/remembered, remembered, felt, informed/told, felt/thought, agreed/felt, noticed, claimed, discovered/found, accepted

3 i a/b/e/g   ii c/f/h   iii c/f/h   iv a
  v b/c/e   vi a/d/g   vii b/c/e   viii a/d

4 a begged/pleaded
  b concluded/observed/remarked
  c ordered/warned
  d announced
  e grumbled/mused/reflected
  f advised/insisted/warned

5 i d   ii e   iii a   iv f   v b   vi c

6 a told me/said
  b warned me/said
  c promised me/said
  d assured her/said
  e reassured him/said
  f assured us/promised us/said
  g informed us/said
  h told him/said

7 i b,c,e,f   ii a,b,d,e   iii a,b,d,f

8 a Karen urged Anthony to apply for the job.
      Karen suggested that/proposed that Anthony should apply for the job.
  b The headmaster recommended/suggested that Peter should go to university.
      The headmaster advised Peter to go to university.
  c The boss asked/instructed Jane to give him the latest reports.
      The boss requested/directed/demanded that Jane should give him the latest reports.
  d David suggested/proposed that Jenny should pop in when she is/was in the area.
      David urged Jenny to pop in when she is/was in the area.
      David expects Jenny to pop in when she is in the area.

9 a It is guaranteed
  b It has been estimated
  c It is/has been predicted
  d It is rumoured/reported
  e It is assumed/rumoured

11 a is guaranteed to work for a year.
  b were expected to arrive last week.
  c has been predicted for tonight.
  d are reported to have been injured.

12 i,g at   ii,h to   iii,f at   iv,b to
  v,a to   vi,c to   vii,i at   viii,e to
  ix,d to

13 "... As for the present position, I agree with a good deal of what the Dean says. But I don't consider this is the right time to act. I know this long wait hasn't improved some of our tempers. But it won't be much longer. Speaking as a fellow, I don't see any alternative to waiting. I didn't quite understand the Dean's suggestion. I do not know whether he thinks that other names ought to be canvassed now. Speaking as a candidate, I can't be expected to accept the view that other names ought to be considered at this late stage. I hope that the Senior Tutor agrees with me."

14 believed/thought, announced/revealed/said, believed/expected, announced/hinted/revealed

15 On drugs we asked two questions: "Which of the following drugs have you tried?" and "Which drug do you think most dangerous in terms of the effect it has on society?" Overall, 65 per cent claimed to have tried cigarettes, 17 per cent cannabis, 6 per cent solvents and 89 per cent alcohol. Two per cent claimed to have tried heroin (the bravado factor, you might suppose, being cancelled out by the reticence factor; 7 per cent refused to answer this question). But, worryingly, 3 per cent of under-14's claimed to have sampled it; and a huge 85 per cent of under-14's reckoned to have tried alcohol, with only 8 per cent thinking it harmful. Only four in ten of the over-19's thought heroin most harmful. The government clearly has a lot of educating to do.

Chapter 8

1 Co-ordinating conjunctions : a,d,f
Subordinating conjunctions : b,c,e

2 i a,b,e,f   ii a,b,c,d   iii b,c,d,e

3 a All the time I was in France, I only saw three boys I knew.
  b Whenever he wrote to me I failed to answer.
  c As soon as I heard the door slam I rushed downstairs.
  d Hardly had I walked through the door than the phone rang.
  e Ever since he left university he has been teaching./Ever
     since he left university he has been a teacher.

4 a since
  b Whenever
  c long before
  d now that
  e The last time
  f when

5   i   a,c,e,f,g
    ii   a,c,d,f
   iii   b,d,h,i
   iv   a,c,e,f,g
    v   a,d,f,g
   vi   b,d,h,i
   vii   a,c,e,f,g
  viii   a,d,f,g
   ix   b,d,h,i

6 Lines 2 to 6 of the poem all contain conditional clauses.

8

Hillside Cottage,
Tumbledown Row,
Old South Downe

28 February

Dear Sir,

I am writing to you *as/because* we have still not received a reply to a letter we wrote to you more than two weeks ago. I regret to say that I am *still* not satisfied with the work done by your company.

Your workmen came yesterday *because* you sent them to rectify their mistakes. They did, in fact, attempt to repair the roof, and *since/as* this has been done I should feel happier. However, they made no attempt to replumb the extension I am still extremely dissatisfied.

They say they have done the plumbing, and *since/as* there are pipes under the floorboards, this is true, but these pipes do not work. My suspicion is that they have not been correctly joined, and we have buckets ready *just in case* water starts dripping through the floor of the extension down into our living room! In addition we have switched the electricity off *in case* the faulty wiring causes a fire!

We are looking forward to hearing your comments on this.

Yours faithfully,

Mrs B. O'Brien

9

BODGER & SON
ALL FALLE DOWNE

Tom – please pass this message on to Dick and Harry. Mrs O'Brien has written *again* – please put your work right immediately *so that* she stops writing to me. I've been to see the extension in question and I agree with what she's said. She's *so* dissatisfied that I wouldn't be surprised if she took us to court – but I don't blame her – the work is *so* bad *that* we'll all be out of a job if you don't do better! It was *such* a straightforward job *that* I can't believe such a mistake has been made.

So please get things sorted out, *or else* I'll have to see Dick and Harry myself. Please get in touch with them immediately.

10 *Mr Bodger:*
Hello - Mrs O'Brien? Bodger here. I trust that the men have completed the work to your satisfaction now.

Mrs O'Brien:
Well - they've been working, though I wouldn't say it was right. Although you've made an effort to get the work done, it's hardly adequate. And to be honest, we feel we should get our money back, even if you feel you can offer to do the work yourself.

Mr Bodger:
What's the problem now?

Mrs O'Brien:
I think you'd better come and see for yourself. What really annoys me is that in spite of the fact they've come back again and again, it's still far from perfect. They work just like anyone else, except that they take breaks every 5 minutes. You may find that whereas other customers don't mind, we've had enough.

Mr Bodger:
I'll come over and inspect the work right now.

11 *Mrs O'Brien:*
Well, Mr Bodger I can't thank you enough for giving up all your time. It looks even better than we'd hoped. You've done the work exactly as we wanted.

Mr Bodger:
I'm sorry - I can only apologise for the trouble you've had. I can't work out why they behaved as they did. I feel as though I have no control over their work. Wherever I've looked, they've made mistakes.

Mrs O'Brien:
Some of this work, just as you yourself said, should have been quite straightforward. Now it's much as I would expect in my own house. I'm not sure whether they'll get any more work from me. They've behaved as if they don't want a job, that's for certain.

12   **i** c   **ii** f   **iii** e   **iv** a
     v d   **vi** g   **vii** b   **viii** h

13

a And <u>although cast adrift while he pursued other interests</u>, other plans, she was waiting for him, <u>as one waits for an enemy</u>; <u>once they met</u>, she would, by dint of insult and outrage, reawaken the fury that had once been between them.

b They are dark caves. Even <u>when they open towards the sun</u>, very little light penetrates down the entrance tunnel into the circular chamber. There is little to see, and no eye to see it, <u>until the visitor arrives for his five minutes</u>, and strikes a match.

c <u>Only when he reached Liverpool Street</u> was he aware of hunger. He bought himself a coffee and roll <u>before catching the train home</u>. It was nearly four <u>before he put his key in the latch</u>. ..... <u>Although it was still early</u>, he felt very weary and his legs ached.

14 Defining clauses : b,d,e,g   Non-defining clauses : a,c,f

15 **a** The postman who/that has dark hair is always early.
 b The postman who/that I like the best always waves and smiles.
 c The computer which/that works best costs £800.
 d The computer which/that I've recommended is very efficient.

16 **a** The garden, which is south-facing, is almost 100 metres long.
 b The garden, which we landscaped ourselves, is very green at the moment.
 c My mother, who visits me regularly, helps look after the children.
 d My mother, who/whom the children love, keeps them amused for hours.

17   **i**   a,b,e,f
     ii   a,b,c,d
     iii   a,b,d,e
     iv   a,b,c,e

18 **a** I gave the letter to George, who then posted it for me.
 b You might find the exam too difficult, in which case do what you can.
 c A friend told her to improve her diet, at which point she made a huge effort to eat more healthily.
 d She gave up cigarettes last year, by which time she had been smoking for ten years.
 e Some people can't swim, which means they may get nervous on a boat.

19   **i** f   **ii** g   **iii** b   **iv** h   **v** i
    vi j   **vii** e   **viii** a   **ix** d   **x** c

20 **a** John gave us the documents, neatly folded and filed.
 b Absolutely baffled, I reread the extract.
 c The children sat down obediently, their eyes on the food.
 d She was looking unkempt, her skirt crumpled and creased.
 e Shocked by the news, I tried to work out what needed to be done.

21 **a** but/yet   **b** or   **c** but/yet
    d and   **e** but   **f** or

22 **a** Both my husband and I drive estate cars.
 b Neither John nor Juliette was there.
 c I felt both physically and mentally exhausted.
 d You can put it both in the oven and in the microwave.
 e I was both disappointed and hurt.
 f She felt neither delighted nor upset.

Chapter 9

1

it	=	the Re-education Committee
She	=	The cat
one	=	(doesn't refer back)
her	=	the cat's
She	=	The cat
them	=	the sparrows
all	=	(doesn't refer back)
her	=	the cat's
the	=	the sparrows already mentioned
their	=	the sparrows'

2 **a** This, These
b that, that
c This, this, That

3 **a** the former, the latter
b previous
c above
d thus
e then
f in this way

4 **a** Her interpretation of the film was interesting.
Her (personal) view of the film was interesting.
b He gave us a good assessment of the situation.
His evaluation of the situation was good.
c I've come to the conclusion that this is no good.
I've reached the decision that this is no good.

5 **i** f **ii** d **iii** b **iv** c
v h **vi** g **vii** a **viii** e

6 **a** excerpt, extract, passage, phrase, quotation, sentence, text, words
b excerpt, extract, instalment, item, letter, paragraph, section, sentence, table, text, words
c example, excerpt, extract, item, letter, paragraph, passage, phrase, quotation, sentence, statement, summary, table, text, words
d example, item, table, words
e chapter, example, item, paragraph, sentence, summary, table, text, words
f example, item, phrase, quotation, sentence, table, text, words
g item, paragraph, passage, quotation, sentence, statement, table, words

7 **a** expect/hope/think so
b hope so/not
c expected/told, do so
d suppose so

8 **a** matching, contrasting
b comparable
c unrelated
d opposing, compatible
e adjacent

9 **a** this **b** such **c** the following
d This **e** The following **f** these
g next

10 **a** this/the following/the next
b following/next
c below
d such
e These

11 **a** is **b** did **c** had
d did **e** wouldn't **f** can

12 **i** b,d,e **ii** a,d,f **iii** b,e,f **iv** b,c,f

13 **i** c,f,g **ii** b,d,g **iii** a,e,i **iv** d,g,h

14 **a** So was I. / I was too. / What! / Really?
b Really? / Didn't you? / I didn't either! / Neither did I!
c Definitely. / Really? / What? / So had I. / I had too.
d Wouldn't you? / Really? / Neither would I. / I wouldn't either.

Chapter 10

1 a focus on what happens, processes and scientific experiments
b agent unknown
c obvious who the agent is
d as a. above
e people in general are the agents

2 a The soup was served with a ladle. / A ladle was used to serve the soup.
b This decision has been debated by a number of teachers.
c Good blooms will be developed by frequent watering.
d You're being called.
e It is said that fibre is good for your health.

3 i with e   ii in d   iii in a   iv by g
v by f   vi with c   vii with b

4 a is … rationed
b has been suspended
c was deafened
d were fined
e is/has been … acclaimed
f was rained off

5 More rain is forecast for the next few days.
Last night all shipping in the English Channel and the Solent was advised to seek shelter and cross-channel ferries were hit. Many roads remained closed all over the country, and rail services, particularly in the west, will be disrupted for several days.
Four trainee marines were treated for hypothermia after being airlifted by RAF helicopter from Dartmoor. The cost of damage from the floods this winter is now being counted in millions in the South-West and Wales.

6 a It was Francis who first told her the news.
b It is my brother who is ill, not my sister.
c What amazed me was their generosity.
d What they want is more money.
e All you need is an open mind on the subject.

7 a refers to a whole situation or fact that has been implied
b refers forward to a 'to' - infinitive clause
c used to talk about the weather
d refers to a whole situation
e introduces a comment

9 i b   ii e   iii a   iv d   v f   vi c

10 a saying that something happened
b literary
c saying that something exists
d saying that something exists
e saying that something happened
f spoken - contracted form

11 i d,e   ii a,b   iii b,d   iv c,e   v c,d
vi d,e   vii d,e   viii a,b,d   ix d,e   x a,b,d

12 a Rightly, wrongly
b kindly
c generously
d carelessly/foolishly
e bravely/cleverly/correctly

13 a Officially, unofficially
b in theory, in practice
c apparently/ostensibly/supposedly, actually/really
d allegedly/apparently/seemingly
e Nominally /Ostensibly/Supposedly/Theoretically
f probably

14 i e   ii i   iii j   iv a   v h
vi c   vii b   viii g   ix d   x f

15 a At a rough estimate, there are about 70 students.
b They come to classes every day, as a rule.
c For the most part, they enjoy doing grammar.
d All in all, they're very willing.

16 i d   ii c   iii e   iv b   v a

17 a He has actually overspent his budget.
b The hotel didn't even have a restaurant.
c I really loved the trip on the river.
d It is very kind of you, to say the least / to put it mildly.
e For heaven's sake, don't look at me like that.

18 i f   ii a   iii b   iv c   v d   vi e

19 a just/only/purely/solely
b purely/simply/solely
c just/only
d exclusively/purely/solely

20

INDICATING AN ADDITION	INDICATING A PARALLEL	CONTRASTS AND ALTERNATIVES
at the same time furthermore moreover	by the same token likewise similarly	by contrast nevertheless on the contrary
CAUSES	INDICATING A SEQUENCE IN TIME	ORDERING POINTS
accordingly thereby thus	meanwhile simultaneously subsequently	in conclusion secondly to sum up
INDICATING A CHANGE IN A CONVERSATION	EMPHASIZING	
by the way incidentally you know	even positively to put it mildly	

21 a guarantee
b sentence
c deny
d propose/second
e forgive

22 a hasn't he?
b didn't it?
c will you?
d aren't I?
e will you?
f shall we?
g won't you?
h does it?

Reference Section

1

/s/	/z/	/ɪz/
banks	bags	batches
cloths	breeds	branches
kits	drains	foxes
pits	girders	flashes
	spears	houses
		losses

2

a loaves	**b** sparks
c analyses	**d** pitches
e mice	**f** badges
g nuclei	**h** fleas
i firemen	**j** strata
k discs	**l** oxen
m flamingos/flamingoes	**n** crumbs
o classes	**p** echoes
q indexes/indices	**r** flies
s radii	**t** vertebrae

3
a my parents' dog
b my mother and father's house
c St Mary's school
d the children's bags
e three people's passports
f women's rights
g Julie's camera

4

/s/	/z/	/ɪz/
Beth's	Rod's	Liz's
Luke's	Sue's	Madge's
Ralph's	William's	Ross's

5

a 63,127	**b** 7,384	**c** 3,429,860
d 179,324	**e** 815,699,253	**f** 1,634,592

6
a twenty first (21st)
b forty fifth (45th)
c third (3rd)
d a hundred and twenty second (122nd)
e ninety ninth (99th)
f fifty eighth (58th)
g twentieth (20th)
h three hundredth (300th)

7
a a half ; 50%
b a quarter ; 25%
c three quarters ; 75%
d four hundredths ; 4%
e seven tenths ; 70%

8

/s/	/z/	/ɪz/
baths	arrives	buzzes
leaps	drags	finishes
loots	foregoes	fixes
picks	infers	judges
puffs	speeds	reduces

9

a	skipping	skipped
b	stowing	stowed
c	spotting	spotted
d	manning	manned
e	chewing	chewed
f	distilling	distilled
g	disagreeing	disagreed
h	conferring	conferred

10

/t/	/ɪd/	/d/
amassed	cried	alluded
enriched	enlivened	invented
kipped	niggled	raided
mashed	ratified	sprinted
peaked	tickled	spurted

11 bet burst cast cost cut hit hurt let put quit set shed shut spread thrust

broadcast forecast miscast typecast undercut beset reset typecast

12

a shoot	**b** hide
c bind	**d** thrust
e ride	**f** tread
g stand	**h** stride
i tell	**j** do
k understand	**l** forbid

13
a overran/has overrun
b will underwrite/have underwritten/are underwriting
c underwent
d misheard
e has outgrown
f overslept
g have misspelt
h overheated

14

a has	**b** is
c had	**d** had; would

15
a simple present
b past continuous
c past perfect
d present continuous
e present perfect
f simple past
g future continuous

16
a simple present
b past continuous
c future perfect
d past perfect
e present perfect

17

a shyly	**b** fortnightly
c easily	**d** gently
e straight	**f** tragically
g purposely	**h** satisfactorily
i outright	**j** deeply
k eerily	**l** freelance
m crookedly	**n** wryly